MW00932188

STOP OVERTHINKING TO FINALLY GET STUFF DONE

HOW TO REFRAME YOUR MINDSET SO YOU DON'T
WASTE TIME WORRYING ABOUT THINGS THAT
DON'T MATTER AND DIRECT YOUR ENERGY
TOWARD RESULTS

THINKNETIC

CONTENTS

Get 100% Discount On All New Books!

Get ALL our upcoming eBooks for FREE
(Yes, you've read that right)
Total Value: $199.80*

You'll get exclusive access to our books before they hit the online shelves and enjoy them for free.

Additionally, you'll receive the following bonuses:

Bonus Nr. 1

Our Bestseller
Critical Thinking In A Nutshell
Total Value: $9.99

Did you know that 93% of CEOs agree that THIS skill is MORE IMPORTANT than your college degree?

Here's just a fraction of what you'll discover inside:

- The critical thinking framework developed by two of the most experienced critical thinking scientists of all time - and how to make it your own
- The 7 qualities of a critical thinker - how many do you have right now?
- How to shortcut the famous Malcolm Gladwell "10,000 Hours Rule" to become an expert critical thinker, fast

"This book is a good primer for the beginner and a good refresh for the expert who wants to bring more critical thinking into their problem-solving. Easy to read and understand, buy this book."

(Kevin on April 19, 2021)

"This book is unlike any other on Critical Thinking. The author puts an entirely new twist in critical thinking. Very easy to understand. Give it a read and see for yourself."

(Knowledge Seeker on April 16, 2021)

"The explanations are straight forward, sensible and usable with some interesting ideas about how this can be taught or learned."

(Dave Crisp on April 14, 2021)

"This book is an excellent resource to form the structure to practice critical thought. The concepts are clear and to the point. I would recommend this book to anyone wanting to adopt more rigorous and honest intellectual habits."

(Andrew Taegel on June 26, 2021)

"Loved the book. It was also provided a fantastic explanation of Richard Paul's model. Highly recommend. Only drawback, I would like to see the authors name to determine their qualifications."

(dcNatz on August 5, 2021)

Bonus Nr. 2

Our Bestseller
The Intelligent Reader's Guide To Reading
Total Value: $9.99

Why do I need to read or remember anything? Everything I could possibly want to know is on the Internet.

Here's just a fraction of what you'll discover inside:
- Why reading books is a must-have component in the digital age (and how to make it a lifelong habit that will change your life forever)
- The four game-changing techniques that will take your reading skills to the next level and help you read smarter, not harder
- How to ask a book questions (and get the answers you want)

"This is by far the best set of tools and strategies that I've read on improving reading. This is what I wished had been taught in Junior High. I've learned them by trial and error and see how they all fit together."

(Michael McFarren on January 26, 2023)

"I consider this book as the modern version of Mortimer Adler's classic <<How to Read a Book>>. As is standard in the Thinknetic series, there are short chapters with summaries and action items. I think the presentation is thorough and enlightening, hinging on the central question - Why am I reading this book? Outstanding!"

(Ed R. on February 10, 2023)

"The Intelligent Reader's Guide excels in the helpful and easily applicable tools and methods for best reading and internalizing a book. I've taken short courses on how to best read books. The courses don't compare to this powerful resource. This book is a must buy for the student, teachers, and the casual reader for enriching the reading experience."

(Michael K.J. Popovici on February 1, 2023)

"I have read books of all types of genres for years. This book has clear and precise ways of reading to help one gain the most benefit out of their reading experience. I recommend all give it a good look there is something to learn for all."

(Raymond E. Smith on March 2, 2023)

Great! 👍 It makes reading a book like listening to someone willing to explain things to you. Reading is not anymore an isolating task but an adventure with one who shows new worlds and different people in life. Quite a helpful book!

(Susie on March 12, 2023)

Bonus Nr. 3 & 4

Thinking Sheets
Break Your Thinking Patterns
&
Flex Your Wisdom Muscle
Total Value Each: $4.99

A glimpse into what you'll discover inside:

- How to expose the sneaky flaws in your thinking and what it takes to fix them (the included solutions are dead-simple)
- Dozens of foolproof strategies to make sound and regret-free decisions leading you to a life of certainty and fulfillment
- How to elevate your rationality to extraordinary levels (this will put you on a level with Bill Gates, Elon Musk and Warren Buffett)
- Hidden gems of wisdom to guide your thoughts and actions (gathered from the smartest minds of all time)

Here's everything you get:

✓ Critical Thinking In A Nutshell eBook **($9.99 Value)**
✓ The Intelligent Reader's Guide To Reading eBook **($9.99 Value)**
✓ Break Your Thinking Patterns Sheet **($4.99 Value)**
✓ Flex Your Wisdom Muscle Sheet **($4.99 Value)**
✓ All our upcoming eBooks **($199.80* Value)**

Total Value: $229.76

Go to thinknetic.net for the offer!

(Or simply scan the code with your camera)

SCAN ME

*If you download 20 of our books for free, this would equal a value of 199.80$

WHAT READER'S ARE SAYING ABOUT THINKNETIC

"Thinknetic embodies an innovative and progressive educational approach, expertly merging deep academic insights with contemporary learning techniques. Their books are not only insightful and captivating but also stand out for their emphasis on practical application, making them a valuable resource for both academic learning and real-world personal development."

—Bryan Kornele, 55 years old, Software Engineer from the United States

"Thinknetic's works provide a synthesis of different books giving a very good summary and resource of self-help topics. I have recommended them to someone who wanted to learn about a topic and in the least amount of time."

—Travvis Mahrer, BA in Philosphy, English Teacher in a foreign country

"I have most of the ebooks & audiobooks that Thinknetic has created. I prefer audiobooks as found on Audible. The people comprising Thinknetic do an excellent job of providing quality personal development materials. They offer value for everyone interested in self-improvement."

—Neal Cheney, double major in Computer-Science & Mathematics, retired 25yrs USN (Nuclear Submarines) and retired Computer Programmer

"Thinknetic is a provider of books regarding mental models, thought processes, organizational systems, and other forms of mental optimization. The paradigmatic customer likely is to be someone in an early- to mid-career stage, looking to move up the ranks. Ultimately, though, the books could be of use to everyone from high school students to accomplished executives looking for ways to optimize and save time."

—Matthew Staples, 45, Texas (USA), Juris Doctor, Attorney

"I have been reading books from Thinknetic for a while now and have been impressed with the CONDENSED AND VALUABLE INFORMATION they contain. Reading these books allows me to LEARN INFORMATION QUICKLY AND EASILY, so I can put the knowledge to practice right away to improve myself and my life. I recommend it for busy people who don't have a LOT of time to read, but want to learn: Thinknetic gives you the opportunity to easily and quickly learn a lot of useful, practical information, which helps you have a better, more productive, successful, and happier life. It takes the information and wisdom of many books and distills and organizes the most useful and helpful information down into a smaller book, so you spend more time applying helpful information, rather than reading volumes of repetition and un-needed filler text.

—Dawn Campo, Degree in Human psychology and Business, Office administrator from Utah

"I'm a subscriber of Thinknetic for over a year now. I would recommend Thinknetic books to anyone who wants to improve their understanding of cognitive behavioural therapeutic principles."

—Sunil Punjabi, Maharashtra (India), 52, PhD, Psychologist

"I wanted to read some books about thinking and learning which have some depth. I can say "Thinknetic" is one of the most valuable and genuine brands I have ever seen. Their books are top-notch at kindle. I have read their books on learning, thinking, etc. & they are excellent.

—Sahil Zen, 20 years old from India, BSc student of Physics

"I came to know about Thinknetic from the Amazon Kindle. There were recommendations for some of the Thinknetic books. Found every book very interesting. I really loved it. Subscribed for the free material which was delivered right into my inbox. Since then, I have been a fan. I couldn't buy the books... since am in a situation. But as soon as I get a sufficient amount, I plan to purchase some nice titles that piqued my interest. I recommend the books to everybody who wants to live a life free from all sorts of mental blocks that reflect in real life. These books are definitely the lighthouse, especially for those crawling through the darkness of ignorance. I wish Thinknetic all the best."

—Girish Deshpande, India, 44, Master of Veterinary Science, working as an Agriculturist

INTRODUCTION

What was the worst nightmare you've ever had as a kid?

For some children, this could've been a monster. For others, it could've been a major issue in the family or a public embarrassment at school. I can understand those nightmares, but I don't remember having anything similar.

It took me several decades to make sense of my strange terrors.

I remember waking up screaming at age seven, with beads of cold sweat running down my face. For the next half an hour, I couldn't calm myself down, let alone describe that dream to my parents. So, what was it all about?

I'm outside, walking to the local market down the street. After a while, I notice I'm not getting anywhere. The store appears to be slowly drifting farther and farther. I hurry. I start running, but I'm still getting nowhere. Eventually, the street around me speeds up, and at a higher pace than I do. I can't keep up, no matter how hard I try! The trees and buildings smudge into a colorful motion blur. The wind howls in my ears. I run until I'm out of breath—then wake up gasping for air and choking on my tears.

This exact dream repeated itself every few years, then stopped. For good, I hope.

A decade later, I was reading Lewis Carroll's *Through the Looking Glass*, the second installment of Alice's adventures.[1] It's a wonderful book, but one scene felt eerily familiar: the Red Queen's race.

There, Alice was running as fast as she could, yet not getting anywhere.

"Here, you see, it takes all the running you can do, to keep in the same place. If you want to get somewhere else, you must run at least twice as fast as that!" said the Queen.

This terrifying concept has stuck with me since as far as I can remember—first as a childhood nightmare, later as the Red Queen's race.

The very idea that you could be putting ALL your energy and resources and STILL not moving forward... It sends chills down my spine. Luckily, that's just an imaginary situation. Right?

That's what I used to believe.

Later, I realized I was a chronic overthinker and finally connected all the dots. See if this sounds familiar…

You spend hours upon hours "working" on a project… But see little to no progress. You brace yourself for dozens of outcomes and problems… But they keep popping up in your mind at an ever-increasing pace.

You can't keep up. You're overwhelmed. Stuck.

In this case, moving forward feels impossible. It takes all your inner resources to just stay in place—in the insanity of the Red Queen's race.

Now, here's the good news: It's possible to escape it, and I want to show you a proven route.

In this book, I'll share the techniques and strategies that I found to be the most effective for dialing down my overthinking. Some of them helped me finish medical school, and others came in handy while I switched careers from anesthesiology to writing.

Did these strategies "cure" my overthinking? Not exactly.

Overthinking isn't a medical condition on its own. It doesn't have to be cured, but to be *managed effectively*. Consider it a mental habit that brings trouble only if it spirals out of control. When this happens, you may struggle with impaired productivity, sub-optimal performance, a tremendous waste of resources, and a wide range of mental health issues.

But what's the alternative, if you learn to manage your overthinking better?

Your energy will be turned into tangible progress, not just frantically running in place. You'll be able to work consistently and perform at a high level without sacrificing mental health. Most likely, you'll be on the path to a more fulfilling, yet considerably less stressful life.

Regardless of your specific line of work, I'm sure that the concepts in this book will help you reduce overthinking and empower growth. Psychological principles, time management tips, productivity hacks, mindset shifts— we've got an exciting journey ahead!

And the best part?

You'll receive exercises and prompts after every chapter. If you put them to good use, I'm confident that you'll see tangible results. With proper focus and practice, overthinking will become much less of an obstacle to your productivity by the time you reach the last page.

We'll get there, but even the longest journey begins with a single step.

So, let's start walking.

Ivan Kokhno

1

YOUR BRAIN IS A TIME MACHINE

HOW TO TRAVEL TO THE PAST AND FUTURE (AND NOT GET STUCK THERE)

Your brain is a time machine.

It perceives, measures, and tells the time to control and fine-tune the intricate machinery of organs inside you. For example, consider how it orchestrates all your circadian rhythms—events that happen at roughly the same time every day.

- Every morning between 7 and 8 a.m., your body produces a spike of the hormone cortisol which helps you wake up and get ready for the day's challenges.
- At night, your cortisol levels drop, and another hormone enters the stage: melatonin. It triggers sleepiness and helps you wind down for a night of rest and recovery.[1]
- Hunger and fullness also have a circadian rhythm. The evening peak in appetite appears to

be an adaptation to the upcoming overnight fast, dictated by sleep.[2]

Your brain plays a major role in controlling all the processes above, and many more. But that's just barely scratching the surface of the mind's relationship with time.

As a proper time machine, your brain also allows you to travel. Every day, you jump back and forth in mental journeys across the chronoscape. Each trip is a recreation of past events (memories) or a simulation of the future (dreams, worries).

The main purpose of these time travels? To help you make better decisions in the present.

This concept was introduced by neuroscientist and author Dean Buonomano, who explored the evolutionary significance and psychological consequences of the brain's complex relationship with time.[3]

Without this never-ending mental jumping back and forth in time, humankind would never have invented agriculture, tools, or food preservation. After all, deciding not to eat the whole rabbit that you hunted down today requires you to make a mental trip into the future and consider the consequences of that choice. What if you don't manage to catch anything tomorrow? Wouldn't it be better to save a bit of that meat for later?

If that sounds a bit far afield, let's picture a scenario that's closer to our day-to-day reality.

Imagine you're getting ready to meet a friend for brunch. You throw a glance at your watch. The time is 1:27 p.m. and you've got to decide on the best way to reach your destination. Google Maps says you can take the local bus and reach the place in half an hour. Just in time.

And then—*WHOOSH!* Your time machine of a brain fires up.

You recall how just a week ago, at about this time of the day, you took the same bus. It was overcrowded, barely moving through the city traffic, and hot like a Finnish sauna on fire. You definitely don't want to go through that experience again. You call an Uber and reach your destination in less than 15 minutes.

Your mental time travel to the past helped you avoid an awful trip in the future, and reach your destination in time, in a better mood, and considerably less sweaty.

In a similar fashion, your brain guides you into mental simulations of the future. For example, when you're choosing a birthday gift for someone, you go through all the possible options and imagine how that special person would react to each of them. When the imaginary reaction is particularly joyful—Bingo! You've found the perfect gift.

As you can see, mental time travel is the essence of hindsight and foresight, helping us to navigate even the smallest of decisions effectively. Unfortunately, there is a flip side.

Time travel isn't just useful. It's also dangerous.

Can you get lost in these mental time journeys? Is it possible to get stuck in the past or future, unable to come back to your own time?

Absolutely. And not just possible, but even quite easy to do. You've probably fallen prey to this temporal trap dozens, if not hundreds, of times before.

If you haven't guessed it already, it's overthinking.

Temporal Traps 101

Overthinking is the general term for repeatedly dwelling on the same thoughts, worries, or doubts. People who struggle with excessive overthinking often have trouble making decisions and taking action.

From a medical perspective, overthinking isn't a recognized mental health issue on its own. You won't find a code for it in the International Classification of Diseases (ICD).[4] Nevertheless, overthinking can be an early symptom of a wide range of conditions, including anxiety and depressive disorders.

That being said, overthinking isn't automatically a bad or unhealthy thing. Everyone does it from time to time, in their own way. Do any of these scenarios sound familiar to you?

- Spending an excessive amount of time on a work-related task, polishing every little detail to a level of perfection that's not required.

- Mentally revisiting discussions or arguments from the past, coming up with various ideas of what you should've said at the time.
- Feeling paralyzed before the prospect of getting to know new people, worrying about what kind of impression you would make on them.
- Postponing the launch of a personal project or business over and over, trying to figure out every single detail of the path ahead before you even make the first step.
- Having trouble falling asleep the night before an important meeting or event, imagining everything that could go wrong the next day.
- Choosing the perfect gift for several weeks or even months, going through hundreds of possible options, always discarding them in search of something even better.

None of those situations is pleasant, but they're all perfectly natural. Sometimes, they may even be beneficial. Those extra hours you've put into polishing a minor task at work may not have been too efficient, but sometimes this level of attention to detail could put you on the radar of your boss. The weeks or months in search of the ideal gift may have been draining, but the amount of care and love that you've put into the process won't go unnoticed by that special person.

Overthinking is such a universal habit for humankind that it has spawned a colorful bouquet of synonyms over the decades. You've probably seen a lot of them in books, movies, and media in general:

- Obsessive thinking
- Mental chatter
- Overanalyzing
- Thinking too much
- Beating a dead horse
- Overintellectualizing
- Being a worrywart
- Micromanaging
- Persistent thoughts

Of course, each of those versions explores a particular aspect or way of overthinking. Perhaps, the funniest is the French term *l'esprit d'escalier*, "the wit of the staircase."[5] It refers to a particularly successful remark that comes to your mind too late to be used. Imagine finishing a conversation or argument, going your way, and then thinking of the best comment at the bottom of the stairs as you leave the gathering. Too late!

Portals To The Past, Fissures To The Future

One thing that all forms of overthinking have in common is their tendency to abduct you from the present moment and send you on a hectic time trip, either backward or forward.

From this perspective, there are two main types of overthinking: *ruminating* over the past or *worrying* about the future. In both cases, you could get lost in thought for many hours or even days. That's why the primary danger of these "time traps" is that they steal your attention from the present, impairing action and diluting your presence in current events.

Rumination overthinking is based on an inability to let go of a past event. The intensity and duration of this process usually depend on how important or traumatizing this event was for you.

In most cases, rumination can be described as a relentless barrage of SHOULD HAVEs firing in your mind as it goes through simulations of what you (or others) were supposed to do in the heat of the moment.

After a tough breakup with a romantic partner, some people can get stuck for months or even years, unable to make peace with the separation. As a result, they isolate themselves and can't form new, healthier relationships. They're trapped in an incessant review of what *should have* been instead of building new connections in the present.

In the event of an unexpected lay-off at work, it may be easy to slip into rumination over your previous performance. What *should have* been your attitude? Maybe you didn't show enough enthusiasm? Or maybe you should've worked overtime more often, learned a new skill, or received a new certificate to showcase?

Sometimes, rumination comes without a "should have" component. It feels instead like a broken record of a memory, playing through the same situation over and over again. Usually, it's a hurtful recollection (like experiencing abuse or surviving a car accident), but it can also be a memory of something pleasant (like a fleeting moment of fame or massive luck).

Regardless of the specifics, any type of excessive rumination is detrimental because it undermines your ability to act in the present. Even though everyone does it from time to time, it's the degree that matters. So, is there a way to counteract this process? How do you close a portal to the past? Let's go through a few techniques based on cognitive behavioral therapy (CBT).

Attentional Grounding

If rumination is a portal to the past, attentional grounding is an anchor to the present. It brings you back to reality by intentionally focusing your mind on what you can see, hear, or feel now.

How do you practice attentional grounding? A classic exercise is the 5-4-3-2-1 technique. Go through the list below one point at a time, noting down or naming aloud the following:[6]

- *Five* things you can see (e.g., a cloud in the sky, a book on the shelf, etc.)
- *Four* things you can touch or feel (e.g., the softness of your clothes, a cool breeze blowing from your window)
- *Three* things you can hear (e.g., the city traffic, the

humming of your fridge, your stomach rumbling)

- *Two* things you can smell (e.g., the freshly brewed coffee in your mug, the scent of freshly cut grass outside)
- *One* thing you can taste (e.g., breakfast, mint toothpaste)

This exercise is tougher than it looks. Sometimes you need a good few minutes to focus on your sensations and define exactly what it is that you're feeling—and that's the whole point of grounding! By bringing your mind back to what you're seeing, hearing, or smelling now, you can considerably weaken the grip of the past on your mind.

<u>Cognitive Defusion</u>

Cognitive defusion is a CBT technique for increasing the distance between the thinker and their thoughts, essentially de-fusing (i.e. separating) them.[7]

The goal here is to realize that you aren't your thoughts. You're just experiencing them. Notice and observe as they pop up and dissipate in your mind. Don't fight them, don't entertain them, just let them be.

For example, let's say that you notice you're slipping into rumination over a recent problem at work—an important email that you missed. Instead of mentally dissecting that event and looking at it from all possible angles, just acknowledge that it happened and that you're thinking about it right now. It will pass. You've received and sent emails previously, and you will do so again in the future. Even if this missed email feels special, in reality, it's just one out of thousands that you'll interact with in your life.

Visualization

This technique goes alongside the previous one (cognitive distancing). Essentially, as you imagine the object of your rumination taking form, you increase the distance between you and the thought. Rumination takes place in your head (really close, right?) but you can "take it out" by imagining it as something else, outside of your body and mind.[8]

- That important email that you failed to answer in time? Imagine it as an envelope-shaped cloud drifting away through the sky. It's there, but it's so far away, up high, slowly leaving your field of view.
- After breaking up with someone and feeling unable to move on, you can mentally or physically write your former partner a letter expressing your emotions. Then, tear it to pieces or burn it down. (Just make sure to do this in a safe way.)

Now that we've finished exploring the basics of rumination, the first type of overthinking, let's close these portals to the past and turn 180 degrees. Get ready to explore the parallel universes of what's yet to come as we slip into fissures to the future!

The second type of overthinking, *worrying about future events*, has its own peculiarities and mechanisms. Many of them can be disastrous for your productivity. In the following chapters, we'll go through a range of strategies and techniques to help you perform your best. But first, let's practice what we've already covered.

Action Steps

Practice attentional grounding. Pick a piece of paper or open your favorite note-taking app and write down five things you can see right now, four things you can feel, three things you can hear, two things you can smell, and one thing you can taste. Next time, when you feel that your mind is slipping into overthinking, repeat this exercise to escape that portal to the past and return to the present.

Categorize your time traps. Divide a piece of paper into two sections: Past (Rumination) and Future (Worrying). Note down the most common themes of your overthinking, categorizing them into one of these categories. This exercise could give you some insights into recurring patterns in your overthinking, making it easier to approach the issue.

In the next chapter, we'll tackle a phenomenon that could easily be the most detrimental effect of worrying about the future: analysis paralysis. This mental state can be so debilitating that any progress becomes virtually impossible. You just can't move forward.

Almost as if you've been turned to stone.

Chapter Summary

- Overthinking is the persistent dwelling on the same memories, thoughts, or doubts.
- The two main types of overthinking include rumination over past events and worrying about the future.
- In both cases, overthinking distracts your attention from the present moment, potentially impairing your ability to take action now and live life to the fullest.
- Some techniques that may help with rumination and overthinking include attention grounding, cognitive defusion, and visualization.

2

STUCK IN A DECISION DEADLOCK?

HOW TO SOLVE THE PARADOX OF THE PERFECT HUNTER AND THE IMPOSSIBLE PREY

A ccording to the legend, thousands of years ago the Greek god Dionysus decided to punish the people of Thebes for an unforgivable crime. He sent a giant fox to ravage Teumessus, a region near the glorious city. Besides its size, the magical beast bore another terrifying property: It was destined never to get caught.

Creon, ruler of Thebes, asked the hero Amphitryon to get rid of the monster that had escaped from countless hunters and warriors. Amphitryon, aware of his limitations as a mortal man, decided to tackle this impossible challenge with the help of Laelaps, a magical dog that was destined to catch everything it would chase.

The perfect hunter started chasing the most coveted prey. The one who never misses set his eye on the one who never gets caught. The almighty Zeus noticed the clash of these mutually excluding abilities and decided to solve the paradox by turning both beasts to stone.

Their statues were cast into the stars, where you can still find them illuminating the night sky as constellations. Swift Laelaps is embodied in the Canis Major, and the elusive Teumessian fox is now the Canis Minor. Both lie in the northern celestial hemisphere and shine the brightest in the evening winter sky from January to March.

So, what does this have to do with overthinking?

Life often feels like the ever-elusive Teumessian fox, impossible to grasp. No matter what you do, it always seems to slither its way through your preparations, leading to new challenges, questions, and doubts. It's the impossible prey. But the power of the human mind is astounding as well. Just like the magical Laelaps, the ultimate hunter, it can potentially capture anything it decides to pursue. This clash of absolute powers doesn't result in anything constructive. Both turn to stone, and no progress is made.

In other words, *analysis paralysis* takes place. This is the general term for those times when overthinking impairs our ability to make decisions, act, and move forward—as if we were paralyzed in a recurrent cycle of analyzing our options.

Luckily, that's not always the case. Moreover, overthinking can even be beneficial in critical situations or before making major decisions.

For example, when you are considering a new career path, haste can lead to a massive waste of time and resources. Thinking through more options and running down multiple scenarios in your head could potentially improve your chances of picking the optimal direction to pursue.

When you're looking for a new property to buy or rent, it's hard to overestimate the importance of this decision. This could be a turning point that will define your life for many months, years, or even decades. Spending some extra time and effort considering all the details could save you a lot of trouble in the long run.

However, in most cases, overthinking does more harm than good, as it revolves around issues of much smaller impact, with fewer long-term consequences and lower stakes involved.

Spending a few weeks thinking through your future career or home makes sense. Spending the same time on writing a single email? Not so much.

So where can we draw the line? Here's an interesting strategy on how to make sure we're not going overboard with the analysis and slipping into paralysis.

A Poor Business Decision

In her book *Don't Overthink It*, author Anne Bogel gives an interesting definition of overthinking episodes:[1]

Those times when we lavish mental energy on things that don't deserve it. Those times when we can't seem to think about anything else, even though we know our thoughts are better spent elsewhere.

In other words, the habit of overthinking can be explored from the perspective of return on investment (ROI). In its standard definition, ROI represents the ratio between net income and the investments required to secure it. The higher the ROI, the more you gain from your investment.

Your time, thoughts, and energy are finite resources. Every day, you choose where to invest them. Even if you don't want to make that decision consciously, it's still unavoidable. You will put your time and energy into something. The difference is in what kind of return on your investment you will get from that today, tomorrow, in a year, in a decade.

From this perspective, the goal of picking the right career path or the best house to purchase deserves much more mental energy and time. It's hard to overestimate the impact that those decisions can have on your life, so your thoughts will be very well spent there. Hopefully, the return you will get from those weeks of focused analysis will materialize in years or even decades of a happier, thriving life. That's an example of a high ROI.

Let's compare that to a less intimidating situation. You're a freelancer writing a small blog post for $50... And you spend two weeks polishing every little detail. Way past the deadline. With nothing major at stake. Is this a good investment of your time and energy? If you divide that $50 by the hours that you've spent writing that blog post, what would your hourly rate be? You can imagine just how abysmal the ROI will be in this case.

Of course, this doesn't mean that you should be always hasty or never put any effort into small tasks, leaving all your skills and energy exclusively for the high-reward things in life. The goal is to strive for balance and be smart with your resources.

That's the main danger of overthinking. It's anything but balanced, and it doesn't have any respect for your resources in the present. It lavishly throws them into the past or future, with no substantial return on these investments in sight.

In some cases, the ROI on this could be even life-threatening. Well, at least in thought experiments.

How Equal Options Can Kill A Donkey

Does free will exist? Are all our choices determined by previous events or current circumstances?

The debate on this philosophical question goes way back to Aristotle. Over the centuries, it sparked a lot of metaphors, and one of its most iconic symbols is a donkey. More specifically, Buridan's ass.[2]

Imagine a starving donkey placed exactly midway between two identical stacks of delicious hay. The paradox assumes that since there's no way to make a rational decision between the donkey's options, the hapless animal will not be able to choose. It will starve to death.

This thought experiment was named after the 14th-century French philosopher and priest Jean Buridan, whose ideas of moral determinism it satirizes. In a nutshell, moral determinism can be described as the idea that when faced with two alternatives, man will always choose the greater good. But what about those cases when all options appear equal?

Buridan argued that if the two courses of action can be judged equal, then human will alone cannot break the deadlock. The only rational option is not to choose anything until the circumstances change, and the best choice is clear again.

Later writers made fun of this argument, and that's how Buridan's ass was created. If the choices of a rational being are determined by circumstances that make the best decision obvious, the donkey will be able to choose between the stacks only after something changes in the situation's setting. For example, if one of the stacks becomes bigger or gets closer to the animal. If they don't, the donkey will starve, unable to identify the best course of action.

Luckily, this never happens in real life. No donkeys were harmed in the creation of this paradox. Maybe it's because our options in life aren't always absolutely identical or because there's more to making decisions than rational determinism.

And still, it's safe to say that we all feel and behave like the proverbial Buridan's ass from time to time. Faced with so many options, when all of them look so delicious, we stand paralyzed between them all. Slowly (and figuratively) starving to death due to a lack of action.

Dissecting Analysis Paralysis

Analysis paralysis (also known as decision paralysis) is defined as a state in which overthinking and overanalyzing impair our movement forward by "paralyzing" our ability to make choices and take action. It comes in many shapes and forms and can affect any aspect of your life.

- Wanting to ask your boss for a raise and never even attempting to do it, stuck instead in a recurrent mental rehearsal of your conversation.
- Planning to start a business and postponing the launch for many years, still thinking through all the potential details.
- Writing a book and getting stuck in recurrent rewriting, never satisfied with its structure or flow.
- Planning a vacation trip with your family and not booking the flight or hotel until the last minute, afraid of making a poor choice.

Of course, all of those tasks require planning, effort, and preparation. The problem isn't in thinking them through, but in overthinking that's intense to the point of impairing action.

Negotiating a raise with your boss isn't a definitive one-time event. Prepare your arguments, give it a shot, and if you don't get a positive response—just try again next quarter or year. Having an actual discussion with your management gives you first-hand experience you wouldn't otherwise get from thinking through the matter alone.

Starting a business is a massive step for anyone, but it's not something set in stone. In most cases, it's better to start soon and grow as you go, figuring out all the details as they appear. If needed, you can always go through a rebranding—or just start a new business altogether. The most important part is to get started.

The same logic applies to most situations in life when you feel stuck in overanalyzing. But why does this happen in the first place?

Therapist Emma McAdam describes three main causes for decision paralysis in her blog *Therapy in a Nutshell*:[3]

1. An unprecedented abundance of options to choose from in the modern world. Making decisions is harder than ever because we have more options than ever before.

2. The risk of disappointment and regret in every choice. Lacking the ability to regulate our emotions during decision-making impairs our ability to choose in the first place.

3. The complexity of executive function. Executive function is the general name for all the mental processes required to select, control, and execute behaviors that help us reach our goals. It's the human brain's struggle to make sense of complex and abstract tasks.

The interaction between having an abundance of choices and facing the risk of disappointment hidden in every option has been explored in detail by psychologist Barry Schwartz. In his book *The Paradox of Choice: Why More is Less*, he argues that having too many options has two major consequences:[4]

- It increases the effort and time required to make a choice.
- It often leaves us unsatisfied with our final decision.

The last point may sound counterintuitive. After all, having more options should increase our chances of making better choices and being happy with them, right?

That's the catch. In most cases, there's no single and objective best decision, especially when it comes to everyday situations. The vast majority of our options are more or less equal, each with its own benefits and drawbacks. This absence of an obvious "greater good" leaves us with no clear path to walk, so we tend to postpone making the decision until we gather more information, or something changes in our circumstances.

If that sounds familiar, you're right on. That's Jean Buridan's argument. We're all donkeys from time to time.

For example, think about the last time you had to buy a new phone, laptop, or camera. Hundreds of options from dozens of brands, meticulously reviewed in a multitude of YouTube videos along the lines of *The 15 Best Laptops to Buy This Year*. If you're on a budget, consider these. Looking for something more powerful? Here you go! Oh, and don't forget to check out these extra 2,371 options, each with its own innovative piece of technology. A few weeks later, you're still choosing that laptop. And when you eventually (finally!) buy something, you're never 100% sure it *really* is the best choice.

What if you had watched just a few more video reviews? Maybe you'd have found something even better. What if you picked the wrong laptop, it breaks down next month, and you'll have to go through all that trouble again?

In many ways, life could be so much simpler and easier if there was just one default phone, laptop, camera, career path, raise proposal, or gift to buy for your romantic partner. The argument *"I had no choice!"* is a universal liberator from doubts and regrets. On the other hand, *"I had so many choices!"* puts all the pressure and responsibility on you if something goes wrong. That's the essence of analysis paralysis.

So, is there a way to make this decision-making process easier?

How To Un-Paralyze Yourself

There's no cookie-cutter approach to making decisions in life, but there are a few strategies to keep in mind as you approach every situation.

<u>Follow Your Core Values And Priorities</u>

When facing a complex decision to make, take some time to think about your top priorities in the matter. In some cases, this will be enough to make the decision for you or at least drastically reduce your options.

- What kind of tasks will you do on your new laptop? If you need it mostly to edit documents and write emails, there's no point in considering a $3,000 gaming setup.
- If you're looking for a birthday gift for someone special, try narrowing your search. Focus on the most important qualities of this present. Does it have to be practical? Should it be closely related to a specific hobby or theme?
- When considering how to approach a friend to discuss a recent disagreement, think about your top priority in the matter. Do you want to emphasize your boundaries or apologize for being too harsh? Is your goal to discuss the root of the argument again, now with a cool head, or mitigate the emotional pain of everyone involved? These intentions may overlap, but

focusing on one of them makes it easier to take action.

<u>Allow Yourself To Rehearse And Experiment</u>

In many cases, we struggle to make decisions because they feel intimidating and definitive. It's almost as if we are actors on stage, and we have to play our part to the absolute best of our abilities before an audience of thousands of viewers. That's a lot of pressure.

But what if you'd approach this decision not as the play itself but as a rehearsal? You're polishing your skills and accumulating experience. Even if something goes wrong, you'll just use this knowledge to perform better next time. Your decisions can be experiments, not a finalized performance.

- While discussing a potential raise with your boss, pick one main strategy and stick to it. For example, you could prepare a report with all the things you've accomplished for the company over the last 6-12 months. Talk it through and check their reaction. If you don't secure the raise after that? No problem. Analyze the talk and pick another strategy for your next attempt.
- When you're starting your first business, consider it a form of training through practice. You'll learn a lot as you open and grow your company but don't forget you can always start a new one. And you'll never have to go to square one again,

as you'll have more experience and knowledge with every iteration.

Remember The Risk Of Inaction

Even though any choice comes with a risk of future disappointment, it's important to remember that not making a decision also does. From this perspective, any course of action is better than paralysis, stagnation, and starvation between two piles of hay.

- What do you lose if you don't even try yourself as an entrepreneur? Time, potential opportunities, connections, and valuable experience.
- What about not mustering the courage to approach that interesting person? You're putting at risk the chance of building a wonderful friendship, romance, or creative collaboration.
- What if you never try writing that book you've been carrying in your imagination since your twenties? You won't polish your writing skills or discover how the story *really* ends.

No effort is ever truly wasted. Even if you don't get the exact results you want, you'll reap priceless knowledge and experience for future projects.

There is a time and place for everything in life, including overthinking. It can be useful when you're dealing with potentially life-changing decisions. When a lot is at stake, it makes sense to think a lot, too—and then think some more after that. For day-to-day events, however, the cost of failure is rarely high, so action is more valuable than analysis.

Lower the stakes, dial down the pressure, and act.

Action Steps

Follow your priorities. Next time you find yourself overthinking a specific task, define your absolute top priority in the matter. For a work-related task, it could be the deadline or budget. Try building your actions on this value alone and see if this approach helps you to act.

Experiment first, analyze later. The goal is simple: Treat your next tough decision as an experiment and give it your best shot. After acting, approach the experience as a test with results that you have to analyze. What went well? What didn't? Was it as scary as you've pictured in your mind or maybe it wasn't that bad at all? Overthinking is about analyzing first and (maybe) acting later. Turn this around. If nothing major is objectively at stake, act first and analyze later.

The myth of Laelaps and the Teumessian fox has a beautiful ending. After being petrified by Zeus and cast into the heavens, the magical beasts were able to stay there as glorious constellations on the starscape. In real life, though, analysis paralysis never leads to results worth admiring.

Perfection is elusive and unreachable, just like the magical fox. Not even the ultimate hunter can seize it.

The solution to this dilemma? Pursue productivity instead of perfection. Our next chapter is dedicated exactly to that.

Chapter Summary

- Analysis paralysis is a state in which overthinking impairs your movement forward by "paralyzing" your ability to make decisions.
- The three core reasons for analysis paralysis are the abundance of choices in the modern world, the risk of disappointment within every choice, and the human brain's struggle to make sense of complex or abstract tasks (cognitive functioning).
- According to the paradox of choice, the more options we have the more effort we need to make a decision—and the more likely we are to be unhappy with our final decision.
- Effective strategies against analysis paralysis include reflecting on your core priorities, reframing decisions as experiments, and remembering that inaction comes with risks and regrets too.
- Overthinking may be useful when you face major decisions, and a lot is at stake. In day-to-day situations, when the cost of failure is usually low, overthinking does more harm than good.

3

THE 1% ADVANTAGE

HOW SMALL SHIFTS IN THINKING AND A LOVE
OF FAILURE ARE YOUR PERFECT WEAPONS TO
DEFEAT PERFECTIONISM

T here are habits and personality traits that are *technically* negative but still retain a noble reputation in society. Perfectionism is one of them.

Most people know this attitude can often be detrimental to everyday performance, leading to slow progress, missed deadlines, and lost opportunities. Nevertheless, there's still something self-flattering about perceiving and announcing oneself as a perfectionist.

After all, can striving for perfection be a negative thing? Shouldn't we always pursue the best results possible? How can we settle for a "good enough" output if we expect to reap exceptional achievements?

The arguments above sound fair, but they're also misleading. Like a talented illusionist, this logic diverts our attention to a captivating facade (the desire for greatness and perfection) and away from the unpleasant truth.

But what's the truth? Elizabeth Gilbert, author of *Big Magic*, offers an interesting take on the nature of perfectionism:[1]

> *Perfectionism is just fear in fancy shoes and a mink coat, pretending to be elegant when actually it's just terrified. Because underneath that shiny veneer, perfectionism is nothing more than a deep existential angst that says, again and again, 'I am not good enough and I will never be good enough.*

This manner of thinking operates in absolutes: success or fiasco, fortune or bankruptcy, glory or oblivion. Perfectionism allows no middle ground, and yet that's where most of the growth happens: in the domain of sustainable productivity.

Productivity Vs. Perfectionism

Perfectionism often disguises itself as busyness. The more time and effort it devours, the easier it is to feel as if you are getting somewhere.

A writer who spent the whole day rewriting the same paragraph without progressing further with the narrative *technically* has worked all day. Was this work productive? Not at all. At the end of the day, the book is still stuck in the same paragraph where it was in the morning.

(I've been there quite a few times while writing this chapter. The irony!)

The drive for nothing less than perfection takes an enormous amount of time and energy, but it seldom brings anything in return. Moreover, this attitude often demands sacrifices that go well beyond the immediate scope of work. When a writer dedicates their whole day to obsessively polishing a single paragraph, what are they losing in the process?

- Momentum from previous work
- Sustainable progress toward the end goal
- Peace of mind regarding deadlines
- Time for meaningful rest or connecting with their family or friends

That's a high price to pay for a single paragraph, even a perfect one.

In most cases, it's better to get something done and move on to the next task than endlessly dwell on a single step of the journey. At this point, it's not about reaching perfection but about optimizing the resources we invest in the matter.

Here's how Charles Duhigg, author of *Smarter Faster Better*, explains this concept:[2]

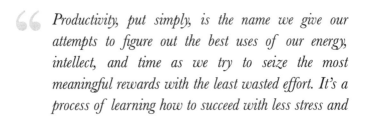

Productivity, put simply, is the name we give our attempts to figure out the best uses of our energy, intellect, and time as we try to seize the most meaningful rewards with the least wasted effort. It's a process of learning how to succeed with less stress and

struggle. It's about getting things done without sacrificing everything we care about along the way.

That's one of the core differences between perfectionism and productivity. The former is largely unreachable, comes with plenty of stress and struggle, and has no limitations on how much of your energy, intellect, and time it can consume without providing meaningful rewards. Productivity is a whole different story. It's a never-ending process of calibration to find the sweet spot where the positive results of your actions are achieved in the swiftest, calmest, and cheapest way possible.

Sounds good? Well, there's a "catch" here.

For any kind of calibration and learning to be effective, you have to take action, and you have to make mistakes. A lot of them. It's all about picking yourself up, learning what you can, and trying all over again,

Picture a baby learning to walk. Their first steps are impossibly clumsy, but fall after fall, they get more efficient, confident, and predictable. One step, fall. One step, two steps—fall again, urgh! The process continues. The baby learns. Soon enough, the little human is running all around the house and finding unexpected adventures in places the parents never imagined.

The same process takes place when the baby is learning to speak, read, write, or ride a bicycle. Without attempts and mistakes, there's no learning. Without learning, there's no optimization.

It's part of the growth process, and we've all been through it hundreds of times. Otherwise, I wouldn't be writing this book, you wouldn't be reading it, and humankind as we know it wouldn't exist in the first place. Civilization was built on mistakes and learning from them—productivity and growth, not perfectionism and paralysis.

How do we find our way back to this attitude?

In a nutshell, it's all about developing the right mindset.

The Tyranny Of Now And The Power Of Yet

You may have heard about the concept of the growth mindset. This fascinating idea was coined by psychologist Carol Dweck in her 2006 book *Mindset: The New Psychology of Success*.[3] Over the years, the concept has become a buzzword, often confused with being flexible, open-minded, or having a positive outlook on life overall. That's not what a growth mindset is about.[4]

At its core, having a growth mindset means believing that you can improve. It focuses more on the effort, the journey, and the learning process. It's the power of not being there YET, but still moving toward that destination.

A fixed mindset, on the other hand, is based on the belief that improvement is impossible. You're stuck with whatever skills, knowledge, or personality traits you have at the moment. It's the tyranny of NOW, unalterable and unavoidable.

The difference between these mindsets affects not only your perception of the challenges you face but also the strategy that you may be more likely to follow in response to them.

In an insightful TED talk from 2014, Dweck illustrated this with the following story.[5]

A group of 10-year-old students were given math problems that were slightly too hard for them. Depending on their mindset (growth or fixed), there were two types of reactions. Children with a growth mindset approached the challenge with enthusiasm. They were excited to use their skills and learn something new along the way. On the other hand, students with a fixed mindset perceived this test as a judgment of their intellect, and failing it felt like a catastrophe.

In several studies, Dweck and her colleagues identified a few common strategies that children with a fixed mindset would be more likely to follow after facing a tough challenge:

- Thinking about cheating on the next test instead of studying more.[6]
- Looking for someone who performed much worse so that they could feel better about themselves.[7]
- Avoiding difficulty, showing less persistence, and putting less effort into future improvement.[8]

In contrast, students with a growth mindset were more motivated in class, studied more, and had higher grades. [6]

The difference is striking.

Having a growth mindset appears to bring universal benefits that can be applied in all areas of life. Sports coaches implement growth-mindset-based practices to motivate athletes, and Microsoft used them to develop leadership-nurturing programs within the company.[9]

So... If having a growth mindset is so beneficial, why don't we all have it?

We do. There's no such thing as pure growth or a pure fixed mindset. Every person has a mix of both.[4] The specific mindset you tap into may depend on the situation. For example, a person may have a fixed mindset when it comes to studying *("I'm just stupid. I'll never get good grades!")* and a growth mindset regarding sports or video games *("I'll definitely improve if I train hard enough!")*

The ratio of your growth to fixed mindset largely depends on your upbringing, education, and previous experience in any given domain. Even such a seemingly minor thing as the specific praise you receive may have a major impact.

For example, a series of fascinating studies reported that praising the intelligence of fifth-graders undermined their performance compared to children who were encouraged for their effort.[8]

When intellect is praised, it's perceived as a fixed trait, part of one's self. You're either clever or dumb; you either passed the test or failed it. There's no place for growth in the tyranny of now. It's a moment frozen in time, and its judgment is merciless.

After failure, children who were praised for intelligence became less persistent in their studies, enjoyed the process much less, and were more likely to describe themselves negatively.

However, when effort is praised instead of intelligence, the focus shifts away from one's traits and skills in the moment. The spotlight illuminates the process of learning and improving. The journey becomes more important than the destination. Children praised for their hard work believed their intelligence and skills could be improved with enough effort.

The belief that intellect and performance are malleable is the foundation of the growth mindset. And it doesn't just help you be more persistent. It leads to measurable results in the long run. Several studies reported that helping students nurture a growth mindset leads to a significant improvement in their grades over the next two years.[6]

So, how do we develop this attitude?

Can you be too late for the growth mindset party? Is it applicable only to children and college students but out of reach for us ancient beings beyond the age of 30?

Reshaping The Adult Brain

For many decades, doctors and scientists believed that the adult brain was incapable of growing new, functional neurons (brain cells).

Why?

On a cellular level, this is explained by the fact that most neurons don't have any centrioles.[10] Centrioles are a type of organelles (the "organs" of a cell, specialized structures with specific functions) that are essential for cell division. Since neurons lack centrioles, they don't divide. A few other examples include red blood cells (erythrocytes) and mature muscle cells. In other words, when you build muscle in the gym, the number of your muscle cells stays the same; they just increase dramatically in size.

The inability of neurons to divide is more of a benefit than a drawback. After all, the human nervous system is extremely complex. Its performance and health are based on an intricate web of interneural connections. Adding an extra neuron here or a few neurons there could easily sever or deform those contacts, altering both their functionality and the information encoded in them. It would be like adding extra letters to already written words, mxaking thiem harfder tlo umnderxstand andd prowcesss. (See?)

Given all the above, it's easy to see why Spanish neuroanatomist and Nobel Prize winner Santiago Ramón y Cajal wrote in 1928:[11]

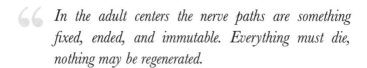

In the adult centers the nerve paths are something fixed, ended, and immutable. Everything must die, nothing may be regenerated.

The good news is that neuroscience has made colossal progress since Ramón y Cajal's words were published. Over the last decades, multiple studies confirmed the presence of neural stem cells in at least three regions of the adult brain: the olfactory bulb, the hypothalamus, and the hippocampal dentate gyrus.[12] Neural stem cells are "master cells" that can develop into young neurons.

In other words, the human brain can grow new cells and form new connections well into adulthood. Sure, the extent of this ability is limited, and the process is rigorously controlled by mechanisms too complex for the scope of this book. But the principle stands. Your brain can improve and reorganize its connections, adapting to life's new challenges.

This phenomenon is called neuroplasticity.

And here's a nice surprise for you: just by learning about this concept and understanding how it works, you're already nurturing a growth mindset. Yep, it's as easy as that. One meta-analysis reported that teaching neuroplasticity to children and adults has substantial benefits:[13]

- Higher motivation levels
- Improved learning performance
- Sharper attention

- Empowered error-correction cerebral mechanisms (the ability of the brain to identify and correct errors)

If we know for a fact that the brain retains its ability to change and adapt well into adulthood, the growth mindset makes much more sense than its fixed alternative.

You can always improve. You can always learn something new, sharpen your skills, and discover exciting opportunities. But that requires taking action, making mistakes, and using them as stepping stones on the path for whatever comes next. The growth mindset is about embracing (and even enjoying) this process of adaptation: the neuroplastic dance of the human brain. Regardless of the outcome, you find value in what you're doing.

In contrast, the fixed mindset focuses on a specific outcome. It's like a snapshot of your brain and skills at a particular moment. There's no process, no growth, and no potential for improvement. If you fail at something, it's a catastrophe. Everything has been for nothing.

When the stakes are this high, perfectionism creeps in. It's an attempt to avoid the fall at any cost. You can't afford to make mistakes in an all-or-nothing situation.

From this perspective, perfectionism doesn't look as good as it did at the beginning of this chapter. It lost its mink coat and fancy shoes. Exposed, it's nothing more than fear of failure.

The alternative is much more enticing, beneficial, and simple: productivity. Get things done, improve a bit, try again, keep improving, keep trying. Enjoy the process.

The Gargantuan Impact Of Minuscule Improvements

Another great concept that can help you adopt a growth mindset is the philosophy of marginal gains. Author of the bestseller *Atomic Habits*, James Clear, gives an in-depth overview of this approach using the success story of cycling coach Dave Brailsford.[14]

He became the performance director of British Cycling in 2003 and the manager of Team Sky in 2010. Following Brailford's lead, British cyclists grew to dominate the track after almost a century of mediocrity.

Between 1908 and 2003, British cyclists won just one gold medal at the Olympic Games. In the 2008 Olympics, the team snatched 57% of all the gold medals available in road and track cycling events (eight out of fourteen). Four years later, during the London Olympics, British riders set nine Olympic and seven world records.

In the first 109 years of the Tour de France, no cyclist from the United Kingdom won the race. Dave Brailsford became the manager of Team Sky in 2010. Fast forward a few years, Bradley Wiggins made history as the first British rider to win the event in 2012. From that year until 2018, the British team won the Tour de France five out of six times.

Brailsford's secret? The philosophy of marginal gains.

Here's how the legendary coach explained the concept in an interview for BBC Breakfast in 2012:[15]

> *If you broke down everything you could think of that goes into riding a bike, and then improved it by 1%, you will get a significant increase when you put them all together.*

That's it. Insanely productive and worlds away from perfectionism.

Instead of leading the cyclists in his team to an abstract concept of perfect performance, Brailsford looked for minuscule opportunities for improvement. This could be anything at all. From testing different massage gels for muscle recovery to improving the riders' technique of washing their hands, it was all fair game.

The results of this approach speak for themselves. When practiced consistently, tiny 1% gains lead to mind-blowing achievements. This is a marvelous embodiment of adopting a growth mindset.

Action Steps

Escape the tyranny of NOW into the power of YET. Think about a skill or domain in which you feel you are underperforming. Maybe you're used to thinking about yourself as unathletic, lacking talent for learning languages, or not cut out for anything creative. Recall the concept of neuroplasticity and make your way to the idea that you can improve if you put enough effort into the matter. You're not athletic YET. You don't know French YET. But you can—if you invest enough time and effort in the matter.

Look for 1% gains. Pick an area in which you want to improve. It could be anything, from a work-related skill to keeping your home tidy. What are the tiniest opportunities for improvement here? Make a list of what comes to your mind and tackle them one by one. Don't seek perfection. Hunt down those marginal gains but do it consistently.

Hopefully, this chapter helped you see perfectionism in a new light. It's a deceitful trait. *"I'm a perfectionist with keen attention to detail"* may sound good on your CV, but in reality, it has little to do with sustainable productivity and growth.

However, even if you know that perfectionism and overthinking are detrimental to your performance, setting yourself free from their grip can be extremely challenging.

In the next chapter, we'll explore why that happens and go through a few techniques that may help you out.

P.S.

I hope you're not afraid of polar bears.

Chapter Summary

- Perfectionism is a fear of failure in disguise. It goes hand in hand with overthinking as a form of worrying about the future.
- Perfectionism is unproductive. It takes a disproportionate amount of time and resources with little to no return. Productivity seeks to find the optimal way to get meaningful results with less stress and struggle.
- Perfectionism is an example of a fixed mindset. It focuses too much on the outcome, not on the learning process. Mistakes are disastrous.
- Productivity is based on a growth mindset, which celebrates the process of learning and improving. Mistakes are an opportunity for improvement.
- Studies have confirmed that the human brain can change, adapt, and form new connections even in adulthood. This concept is called neuroplasticity, and it's the biological foundation of a growth mindset.
- According to the philosophy of marginal gains, even tiny 1% improvements lead to massive results when they are consistent and thoughtful.

4

THE WEGNER EXPERIMENT

WHAT ARE THE WHITE BEARS OF THE MIND AND HOW YOU CAN STOP THINKING OF THEM?

O verthinking is a tough habit to break, especially if you rely mostly on your willpower and thought control. The more you force yourself NOT to overthink, the more persistent and annoying the thoughts can become.

This effect even has its personal symbol in psychology: the white bear.

As you may have guessed, this isn't a random choice. No, there's no scientific evidence that white bears are prone to overthinking. Here's the story.

In 1863, Russian novelist Fyodor Dostoyevsky wrote *Winter Notes on Summer Impressions*, a series of observations during his travels across Western Europe.[1]

More than a century later, one particular thought from this work would become the foundation of a new research domain, the psychology of thought suppression:

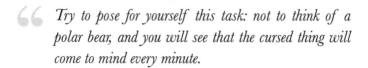

> *Try to pose for yourself this task: not to think of a polar bear, and you will see that the cursed thing will come to mind every minute.*

This quote fascinated American social psychologist Daniel Wegner. In 1987, he decided to test Dostoyevsky's assumption with a simple experiment.[2] The results of his elegant study became the foundation of thought suppression research in psychology.

Each of the 34 participants went through a brief training on how to verbalize their stream of consciousness, meaning to speak out loud all thoughts that came to their mind. Then, each subject was randomly assigned to one of two possible groups. The only difference between them was the order in which they had to perform two experimental tasks.

The *initial suppression group* had to verbalize their stream of consciousness for five minutes, just like they did during their training, with only one exception: They had to avoid thinking of a white bear. Whenever they said "white bear" or thought about one, they had to ring a bell placed on the table before them.

After those five minutes of suppressing the thought of a white bear, participants were asked to perform the opposite task. They had to actively think of a white bear for the next five minutes and ring the bell whenever they mentioned or thought about the animal.

The *initial expression group* performed the same two tasks in the reverse order. They had to speak out loud their stream of consciousness and think about a white bear for the first five minutes. Then, during the following five minutes, they had to suppress the same thought. Just like the other group, they were instructed to ring a bell every time the thought of a white bear popped into their mind.

Here's how often the participants of these two groups rang the bell or mentioned the white bear throughout the experiment's stages:

Initial suppression group

Suppression stage - 2.1 times per minute

Expression stage - 7.35 times per minute

Initial expression group

Expression stage - 5.46 times per minute

Suppression stage - 2.42 times per minute

In other words, participants who tried to suppress thoughts of a white bear ended up thinking about the animal *35% more frequently in the expression stage* compared to the group who was instructed to entertain these thoughts from the beginning! In further studies, this effect has become known as the white bear problem, ironic rebound, or ironic process theory (IPT).

IPT states that when an individual tries to avoid or suppress a certain thought or emotion, a paradoxical effect is triggered. The suppression eventually increases the frequency and intensity of the suppressed thought or emotion.[3]

In the original white bear study, Wegner and colleagues hypothesized that thought suppression results in a growing preoccupation with the thought being suppressed. The process of blocking something out of your mind not only requires considerable focus and energy but also forces you to keep the suppressed thought somewhere in the background. After all, you need it as a reminder of what NOT to think about, right?

It's almost as if all the "approved" thoughts are subconsciously compared with the suppressed ones. *'Is this a white bear? Looks like it isn't, good to go. What about this thought? Does it look like the white bear I'm not supposed to be thinking about? Argh, I did it again…'*

Something similar happens when you try to suppress overthinking as a mental habit. You may succeed briefly at first, sure. However, eventually the question *'Am I overthinking right now?'* starts popping up with increasing frequency.

You start overthinking about whether or not you are overthinking in the first place.

But does this ironic rebound only happen in your thoughts, or does it affect your actions as well?

I Suppress; Therefore, I Smoke

This witty allusion to the thesis *"I think, therefore I am,"* from the French philosopher and mathematician René Descartes, is the name of a fascinating study on thought suppression and behavioral rebound.[4] It turns out that actively fighting off certain thoughts could make us more likely to act on them.

The participants in the study monitored their smoking behavior and self-perceived stress levels over three weeks. In Week 1 and Week 3, all subjects tracked their daily cigarette intake and stress levels. During Week 2, in addition to monitoring their smoking and stress, two experimental groups of subjects either actively suppressed or expressed their thoughts related to smoking. The control group continued monitoring alone, without any thought interventions on Week 2. Here are the instructions that the experimental groups received for the second week:

<u>Suppression group:</u> "Try not to think about smoking. If you do happen to have thoughts about smoking this week, please, try to suppress them."

<u>Expression group:</u> "Try to think about smoking as frequently as possible during the week."

After analyzing the data, researchers found several interesting patterns.

1. The suppression group smoked less during Week 2. However, later in Week 3, the participants smoked

significantly more than the expression and the control group.

2. Perceived stress levels were considerably higher in the suppression group in Week 2 but returned to the baseline in Week 3. Statistical analysis suggests that the increased stress levels during Week 2 weren't a driving force for the increased smoking during Week 3 in the suppression group. In other words, the most likely factor for increased smoking was a behavioral rebound.

3. The expression group didn't smoke more in Week 3, even though they actively entertained their thoughts about the behavior during Week 2.

These findings suggest that thought suppression may seem beneficial in the short term but later leads to a behavioral comeback. In a nutshell, this means a substantial increase in the related behavior after a temporary decline.

According to cognitive behavioral therapy (CBT), human thoughts, emotions, and behaviors are tightly interconnected. Any given component of this triad always affects the other two. From this perspective, it makes sense that IPT affects not only our thoughts or emotions but also our behaviors.

One example of that interaction is the increased smoking after suppressing related thoughts, observed in the study above. Similarly, several other experiments reported that strict dietary restraints can make individuals more susceptible to unhealthy cravings and excessive eating.[5]

The IPT phenomenon may be the simplest explanation for why so many people struggle to break the habit of overthinking. Direct suppression of this process is hardly effective; the thoughts come back with multiplied persistence and intensity.

Chances are, you've experienced this dynamic quite a few times in one form or another.

For example, maybe it was after receiving a vague email from your superior at work, something along the lines of *"drop by my office tomorrow afternoon"* without further details. It's easy to start overthinking the matter, worrying about all the potential trouble that might be coming your way. And if you try to suppress those thoughts, forcing yourself to NOT think about the meeting, you may soon find it impossible to focus on anything else.

It bounces into your mind like a ball off the wall. The harder you throw it, the harder it hits you on its way back. That's the power of the ironic rebound.

To summarize, the white bear problem appears to be a universal psychological mechanism affecting both thoughts and behaviors. Is there a way to break free from its claws?

Effective Strategies Against White Bears

Now that we've explored the mechanism behind the white bear problem, it's time to focus on a few strategies to help interrupt this pattern. Keep in mind, however, that these approaches will not shut off overthinking completely. That's not effective, neither is it realistic. The more you try to suppress the white bear, the stronger it returns.

Instead, think of these techniques as tools that may help you navigate overthinking with mindfulness and intention, potentially reducing stress and increasing your productivity.

<u>Dissect The Problem</u>

The first step to alleviating overthinking is to notice and acknowledge the issue. Then, don't try to block or suppress it; analyze the process and try to get to its root. Here are a few questions that may help:

- Is your overthinking related to the past (rumination) or future (worrying)?
- Is the matter abstract (e.g., aging in general) or related to a specific problem (e.g., knee pain after running)?
- Do you have any control over the object of your overthinking (e.g., a task at work) or is it beyond your immediate agency (e.g., global warming)?

From the perspective of the white bear problem, this analysis process is similar to the initial expression stage in Wegner's experiment. Instead of suppressing the matter and setting yourself up for a future rebound, you actively engage with the issue. You intentionally think about the white bear in a controlled, constructive manner.

In some cases, this process may reveal actionable insights to remedy the situation. For example, imagine you're worrying about your co-worker not answering an important email. After analyzing the matter, you come to a few realizations.

Is the problem related to the past or future? You realize that you're overthinking not the unresponsiveness itself, but the potential complications related to the blocked work process.

Is the problem abstract or specific? The task is well-defined, with clear goals and deadlines. You need input from the unresponsive co-worker to move the project forward.

Do you have any control over the situation? You did everything that was in your immediate power but the project's overall progress is still being compromised.

The starting point was an abstract worrying about your co-worker not answering an important email. The endpoint is a clear understanding that there's a specific project being blocked, and you have to find a way to move it forward.

From this perspective, a few actionable steps become clear. For example, you could send another follow-up to the silent colleague, now with a copy to your immediate superior to alert them about the compromised project. Alternatively, you could seek advice from someone else in a similar working position in your team. This isn't always possible, as many projects have so-called directly responsible individuals (DRIs) for critical steps or deliverables, but at least you could gain some extra perspective on the matter.

<u>Tailor Your Approach</u>

After dissecting the problem, form a strategy that best fits the situation. After all, there's no cookie-cutter approach to overthinking. What works for a goal-oriented and fairly specific task (e.g., the ignored email from the example above) may not be as effective for a vague matter (e.g., potential lay-offs without any signs of them). Different white bears require different solutions.

What if you're overthinking an abstract matter, largely out of your immediate control? What if it's a major event from your past, like a decision to switch careers many years ago?

In this case, one option is to *give yourself some time for overthinking.* Instead of suppressing these worries or ruminations, set a timeframe and allow your mind to explore the topic. Instead of suppressing your thoughts ("Don't think of a white bear!") you're putting a time limit on how long you will express them ("Think of a white bear for the next 30 minutes.") You're reversing the stages of Wegner's experiment: from initial suppression (with a following rebound) to initial expression limited in time.

Another idea is to *isolate a part of the problem* and focus on it instead of the big picture. This makes the whole matter much more specific and easier to deal with.

Imagine that you're overthinking your choice of switching careers many years ago. This complex matter has dozens of aspects. If you try to tackle them all at once, the problem may feel overwhelming. Instead, try to isolate just one part of the question and see if there's anything that you could do about it. Then, move on to the next component.

For example, here are a few possible aspects of the switching careers matter that may lead to rumination over your decision:

- The income difference between the two careers. Is there a way to boost your salary in your current position?
- The stress levels. Can you find a way to unwind and relax more effectively after work?
- The predictability of the workload. Do you often have to work overtime or on the weekend?
- The growth potential. Can you think of a few ways to grow in your current line of work? What would they require from you?

Consider Different Viewpoints

In most instances, overthinking comes in a radically negative light.

If it's worrying about the future, you expect plenty of problems and issues to come your way. If it's ruminating over the past, the bitterness of lost opportunities and committed mistakes is unbearable. Here's a different approach to try: *approach the matter from another perspective.*

This doesn't necessarily mean ignoring all the potential challenges of the future or forgetting everything that went wrong in the past. It's not about embracing unquestioning optimism and exaggerated positivity. Instead, the goal is to navigate away from the extremes and absolute, toward a more balanced, rational middle ground.

Here are some questions that may help:

- What can I learn from this experience?
- What would I consider to be beneficial about this?
- Does this open any new opportunities for me?
- Does this liberate me from any previous burden?

For example, losing a job can feel devastating. Focusing only on the negativity of this event is draining, discouraging, and counterproductive. Instead, try to identify potential benefits and opportunities for growth.

- It's the perfect time to update your CV. Who knows, maybe this glow-up will even help you find a much better position.
- Even if your new position would be similar to the previous one in terms of salary or work responsibilities, maybe it could come with other benefits instead. For example, your new

workplace may be much closer to your home, meaning you'll have to commute less.

- While you look for a new job, you'll have a brief period that you can dedicate to catching your breath and getting some well-deserved rest.
- Maybe this is the perfect time to try a new career that you had been considering but putting off for some reason.

Practice Focused Distraction

In one of Wegner's studies on the white bear phenomenon, his team discovered an interesting way to reduce the ironic rebound that happens after thought suppression.[2]

Besides the two original groups from the main study, a third group was introduced. It was a modified version of the initial suppression approach. Here are the instructions that these participants received:

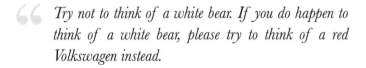

> *Try not to think of a white bear. If you do happen to think of a white bear, please try to think of a red Volkswagen instead.*

It turns out that this intentional distraction was enough to reduce the rebound that happened in the second (expression) stage.

Luckily, the red Volkswagen is just a symbol. Any distraction will work as long as it's intentional and focused. If you feel that you're slipping into overthinking, try shifting your focus somewhere else instead of struggling to block the persistent white bears.

- Watch a captivating movie
- Call a close friend or relative
- Solve a few sudokus or crosswords

Anything that's engaging enough to keep your attention occupied should be able to alleviate the overthinking, at least partially.

Acknowledge And Celebrate Your Progress

In the previous chapter, we explored the concept of the so-called growth mindset. In a nutshell, it's about focusing more on the effort and progress than on specific outcomes.

Guess what? This approach is useful for fending off white bears as well. Instead of focusing on a binary outcome (meaning whether or not you stopped an instance of overthinking) embrace it as a spectrum of possibilities.

Did any of the techniques in this chapter help you worry just a little less than usual? Acknowledge your progress and give yourself a mental high-five.

Remember, praising effort and growth brings better results than focusing on the outcome itself. This activates a self-reinforcing cycle of continuous improvement. No effort is wasted because it always leads to at least some progress being made.

Action Steps

Put your white bear under the spotlight. Recall a recent topic or issue that made you overthink. Instead of blocking it from your conscious mind (thought suppression), actively think about the matter (thought expression) for a specific time. Notice if its grip on your mind weakens after that.

Get yourself a red Volkswagen. Remember that you can partially counteract the ironic rebound effect if you couple the thought suppression with active distraction on something specific. In Wegner's experiment, participants had to focus on a red Volkswagen when they started thinking of a white bear during the suppression stage. What distracter will you choose? Anything could work, as long as you can focus on it whenever necessary.

The possibility of using distracters to fend off unpleasant thoughts or emotions is a fairly universal tool for your mental arsenal. In fact, you may find it useful in many different scenarios that go beyond overthinking and thought suppression.

Brands often add "hold music" for customers to distract themselves while waiting for an operator to answer their call. Installing mirrors in elevators reduces perceived waiting time and boredom, as people can take a few minutes to focus on their hair or adjust their clothes. Watching videos while exercising on a treadmill or cycling machine can help subjects distract themselves from unpleasant exercise-related sensations, improve overall enjoyment levels, and potentially increase long-term exercise adherence.

In other words, the white bear and red Volkswagen interaction can be considered a mental model of sorts. Think of it as a tool at your disposal. Once you know how it works, you can try applying it to a wide range of life scenarios—with varying results, of course, but still worth a shot.

In the next chapter, we'll explore several other mental models for better thinking and sustainable productivity. All of them will be useful against overthinking but have tremendous potential for other areas of life as well.

Let's sharpen a few razors, shall we?

Chapter Summary

- Overthinking is a very tough habit to break, especially through a straightforward approach like thought suppression.
- Studies have shown that active thought suppression may lead to a preoccupation with the thought being blocked. This causes an increase in its intensity and frequency known as ironic rebound, ironic process theory (IPT), or the white bear problem.
- The ironic rebound phenomenon has been observed not only with thoughts but with their related behaviors as well. For example,

suppressing the thought of smoking may increase smoking frequency later. Strict dietary restrictions increase the chance of overeating.

- Focusing on active distracters may be effective in reducing the ironic rebound after thought suppression.
- Other useful techniques include giving yourself time to actively engage with the persistent thoughts, analyzing them to find potential action points, and looking for alternative perspectives on the source of the overthinking.

5

CHOOSE YOUR OWN DECISION-MAKING ADVENTURE

TAKE A SHORTCUT THROUGH THE LABYRINTH OF LIFE WITH 5 KEY MENTAL MODELS TO ACT NOW

S ome life principles feel like magic.

They have an almost unbelievable elegance, simplicity, and universality to them. From finance and productivity to natural phenomena and code errors in programming, these principles work practically everywhere. Could it be that they are some fundamental laws of the universe?

Of course, after some investigation, it turns out that this "magic" has clear mathematical or psychological mechanisms running in the background. This barely makes it any less fascinating.

One of my favorite examples of such wonders is Pareto's principle. It states that *about 80% of the consequences are driven by roughly 20% of the causes.* This is also known as the 80/20 rule or the principle of factor sparsity.

Joseph Juran, an American engineer, stumbled across this principle in 1941 while studying the works of the Italian polymath Vilfredo Pareto. Pareto noticed that approximately 80% of Italy's land was owned by just 20% of its population.[1]

In his future observations, Juran proposed applying this principle to a wide range of matters in life. He also coined the terms "vital few" and "trivial many" to describe, respectively, the small 20% of contributions that drive the bulk of the result and the 80% of other causes that account for just a minor part of the effect.[2]

Here are a few examples of the 80/20 rule in action from different domains of life:

- In any given company, a few best-selling products usually bring in most of the revenue.
- If you are a freelancer, you may notice that in the long run, most of your earnings come from just a few clients.
- Some studies reported using the Pareto principle to estimate maximum rainfall intensity and noted that a small portion of extreme rain events contribute to most of the precipitation.[3]
- Close to 80% of birds observed by birdwatchers belong to just 20% of the common bird species in the area.[4]
- The vast majority of medical errors usually fall into just a few specific types.[5] Addressing them as

a top priority is likely to have the most significant impact on the hospital's overall statistics.

- The CEO of Microsoft once estimated that fixing the top 20% of most frequently reported bugs should be enough to help with 80% of all errors and crashes in the system.[6]

Pareto's principle is a great example of a mental model: a concise representation of a pattern, workflow, or mechanism that helps to simplify complex processes. In other words, it's a cognitive tool that you can use whenever needed—a roadmap for your thoughts.

For example, let's review a few scenarios where the 80/20 mental model could be useful.

On any given day, you're likely to have both major and minor tasks in your to-do list. What are the *vital few* points that, once completed, would bring you the most satisfaction, stress relief, or progress forward? Focus on them before the other, *trivial many*, tasks.

What crucial exercises in your workout routine are likely to bring you the most progress in terms of strength and muscle growth? Most likely, these would be heavy compound movements like deadlifts, barbell squats, bench presses, and so on. Isolation exercises (like biceps curls) are useful too, but they're mostly an addition to the core fundamental movements. If you ever find yourself pressed for time and have to choose just 2-3 exercises for your workout session, compound movements would be the most efficient pick—the vital few.

Pareto's Principle applies perfectly to exercise selection, but sticking to a workout routine can be a whole different challenge. Imagine you've started a workout program that's not bringing the results you want. You're halfway through it, it's not working for you, but you feel obliged to press on simply because you've already invested time and energy into it. In terms of resource allocation, there's another mental model to keep in mind for such scenarios: the sunken-cost fallacy.

The sunken-cost fallacy represents a vicious cycle that makes you more likely to keep pouring resources into something that you're already invested in. The more you invest, the more committed you feel toward the endeavor. That's why the sunken-cost fallacy is usually seen as something detrimental or even dangerous, expressed in the idiom *don't throw good money after bad.* This effect may prevent you from abandoning a failing business because you've invested significant resources into it. The same dynamic may stop you from dropping a workout program that's clearly not doing you any good, simply because you're halfway through it.

However, just like any mental tool, the sunken-cost fallacy can be used to your advantage if you know how it works.

The larger your investments in terms of time, money, effort, and emotions, the more inclined you are to keep putting in the resources. That explains why you're much more likely to finish an expensive educational course than a free e-book. You start by investing the money, and then you become more inclined to follow up by investing your time and attention.

There are hundreds or even thousands of mental models. The more of them you learn, the more diverse and useful your thought toolbox becomes. Thanks to the universal nature of these principles, you can apply them in your work, relationships, and beyond.

Razors, Matrices, And Other Tools Against Overthinking

The beauty and danger of mental models is that they're tools in and of themselves. They can bring you massive benefits if you're aware of how they work. However, they can also lead to a whole lot of trouble if you apply them the wrong way, often unknowingly. You can use a hammer to build a house, but you can also break a few bones with it.

That's why it's so important to expand your horizons, learn more about mental models, and apply them as needed. For example, the sunken-cost fallacy might be preventing you from dropping an exercise routine that's not bringing you results, simply because you're already invested in it. However, just by understanding how this mental model works, you can use it strategically to your advantage. When you're starting a new program, you may find yourself struggling to stick to it. Force your way through the first few weeks, let the sunken cost kick in, and things will get much easier.

In many ways, mental models can help you navigate overthinking. Instead of dispersing your thoughts through the multitude of options and falling prey to analysis paralysis, you can pick a mental tool that best fits the situation. Instead of letting your thoughts wander through countless possibilities, you have a roadmap to guide them.

Let's go through a few examples and their practical use.

<u>Occam's Razor</u>

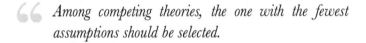 *Among competing theories, the one with the fewest assumptions should be selected.*

Attributed to the 14th-century English philosopher and theologian William of Ockham, this mental model can be distilled into the following principle: The simplest explanation is usually the best one.

Imagine your friend stopped responding to your messages for a few days. If you're prone to overthinking, you could easily come up with dozens of explanations for that. Most of them would be quite elaborate, some even downright exotic. What if your friend slipped on the stairs and broke a leg? What if the Mafia kidnapped them? Or maybe they found an artifact that woke up an ancient evil force from its slumber?

Don't overthink the situation. Life is usually way simpler (and boring) than the picture your overthinking paints. The simplest explanation is often the most likely. Chances are, your friend was just busy with other things. Or maybe their phone is dead. Still far off from breaking a bone or being kidnapped by a gang.

Hanlon's Razor

> *Never attribute to malice that which is adequately explained by stupidity.*

In 1980, Robert J. Hanlon submitted this phrase to a compilation of jokes related to Murphy's Law ("If anything can go wrong, it will.")[7] Since then, Hanlon's razor has become a useful reminder that people can and often do make mistakes. Most of them aren't driven by ill intent. A much more common culprit is a lack of knowledge, experience, or context.

For example, let's say that you're applying for a job. You're great at it. It's the perfect position for you, and you could bring massive value to the company. The working conditions and salary meet your expectations. Everything is perfect. And yet the hiring manager says you're not fit for the position. You don't get the job.

If you keep in mind Hanlon's razor, you can adequately explain the HR's decision with their lack of specialized knowledge. Maybe they have a very vague understanding of the position's technical aspects. Maybe they misinterpreted something in your interview answers because they lack the proper expertise to do so. They're ignorant in this specific context.

Without Hanlon's razor, there's a risk that you could slip into long and exhausting overthinking, considering all the reasons why that hiring manager is just evil. They don't like you. They want you to fail. All that farce of an interview was just downright humiliation.

But would that be true? Probably not. There's much more ignorance in the world than deliberate wickedness.

Satisficing

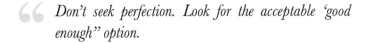 *Don't seek perfection. Look for the acceptable 'good enough" option.*

The term "satisficing" is a portmanteau, meaning a blend of two words: satisfy and suffice. The American political scientist Herbert A. Simon coined the concept in 1956,[8] but he explored the concept much earlier in his 1947 book *Administrative Behavior*.[9]

At its core, satisficing focuses on finding the first acceptable solution instead of wasting additional resources searching for the best one.

Imagine you need to buy a new laptop for work, within a certain budget. There are hundreds of models on the market, from dozens of brands. Which one should you pick? If you follow the satisficing approach, it would be the first laptop you find that:

1. Meets your budget
2. Can handle the bulk of your tasks at work

That's a good enough option.

You could invest days or even weeks into researching the market and the technical specifications of all available options. You could expect to find a laptop that would be 10% or 15% better in terms of performance. But is this slight advantage in performance worth your time and effort? Not necessarily.

In any task or decision, there comes a point after which all further efforts and time start bringing diminishing returns. The good enough option, on the other hand, saves you time and energy that could be better invested elsewhere.

Inversion

> *Instead of seeking brilliance, think about how to avoid failure.*

In most cases, our natural way of thinking is hardwired to look for results, answers, and achievements. Inversion can help to analyze the situation from a different angle, focusing on avoiding failure instead of seeking success.

For example, let's say you're in charge of your company's email marketing. Your task is to send an email campaign today to keep your audience engaged. Maybe you would even make some sales in the process.

If you give way to perfectionism and focus too much on the qualities of that email, overthinking is almost guaranteed. I've been in this situation hundreds of times throughout my career as a copywriter.

"Is this email persuasive enough? Maybe it could be more entertaining? I think the call to action sounds weak, I should rewrite it. Now it sounds too forceful... ARGH!"

What happens if you flip the situation and focus on avoiding failure instead of shooting for the stars? A set of simple objectives becomes clear.

1. Check the factual information, if any.
2. Make sure the email doesn't have silly typos.
3. Don't overthink the offer, call to action, and overall angle. Maybe they don't sound perfect to you as the writer, but they're probably good enough.
4. Send the email. Missing the schedule is often worse than sending a simple campaign. An average email may not bring stellar revenue, but a missed email brings no revenue at all.

Perfection has no limits, but failure is often easy to avoid. Missing the email would be bad. Sending it riddled with typos and misleading information would be awful. But if you cross out the fundamental objectives, you're already in the acceptable zone. Failure avoided!

Mental models are extremely useful because they give you a clear strategy to follow. This eliminates the bulk of the guesswork and helps you streamline your progress.

A related concept uses a mental matrix to structure your tasks or goals. They're somewhat different from mental models but still make useful tools to remember.

The Eisenhower Matrix

On August 19, 1954, the 34th President of the United States, Dwight D. Eisenhower, quoted an unnamed former college president:[10]

> *I have two kinds of problems, the urgent and the important. The urgent are not important, and the important are never urgent.*

This quote became the origin of what we now know as the Eisenhower Matrix. It can be visualized with the help of four quadrants:

	Urgent	Not urgent
Important	Quadrant 1: **DO**	Quadrant 2: **PLAN**
Not important	Quadrant 3: **DELEGATE**	Quadrant 4: **ELIMINATE**

It's a powerful tool that helps you quickly categorize all your tasks depending on their urgency and importance.

Quadrant 1: Emergencies. These are the urgent and important tasks that you have to *do* immediately and personally. Examples include deadlines, problems, and unexpected events. This is the exhausting and stressful quadrant of crisis management and metaphorical (hopefully) firefighting.

Quadrant 2: Focus. This sector is for tasks that are important enough to be done personally, but not pressing enough to require immediate action. *Plan* them intently. In a certain way, this is the domain of calm, focused, meaningful work—or equally meaningful rest, hobbies, and relationships. Ideally, you'd spend most of your time on activities from this quadrant.

Quadrant 3: Interruptions. This category is for urgent tasks with a lower degree of importance. Since they don't demand personal attention, you can safely *delegate* them to an employee, co-worker, or family member, depending on the situation. Later, you may want to reach out to them later for an update on their progress.

Quadrant 4: Time-wasters. The fourth sector is reserved for unimportant, not urgent tasks that tend to slither into our lives and distract us from everything that really matters. For some people, it could be binge-watching Netflix when you're supposed to be working on something important. Others may find themselves scrolling through miles of Instagram Reels instead of going to sleep. Ideally, you should **eliminate** these activities to preserve your time and energy for other, more valuable things.

The Action Priority Matrix

Largely based on the Eisenhower Matrix that we just explored, another useful instrument is the Action Priority Matrix.[11] Just like the previous tool, it helps you choose which activities to prioritize.

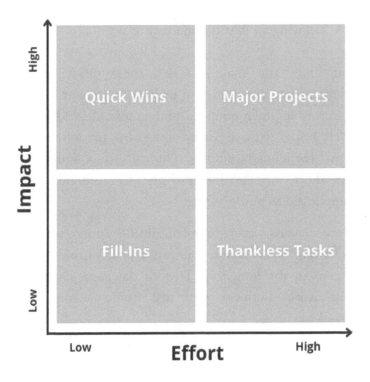

Quick wins are your most attractive tasks and projects. They bring substantial returns for relatively little effort and time. In other words, they have the highest return on investment (ROI) among all your actions. For quick growth, focus on these tasks as much as possible. Depending on your line of work, this could be something similar to:

- Writing and sending an email to your subscribers
- Posting something meaningful on your primary social media platform

- Crafting a short story
- Drawing an illustration for your portfolio

Sometimes you may feel that these quick wins are insubstantial compared to a major project, but their true power is in their quantity and consistency. One email rarely brings massive results on its own, but a hundred of them? For many businesses, that leads to six-figure profits. One short story isn't much of an adventure, but you can compile a dozen into a great book.

Major projects are time-consuming and sometimes downright exhausting—but they can bring colossal returns in the long run. They're the game-changers in your work, business, and art. Some examples may include:

- Writing a novel with complex characters and multiple storylines
- Developing a new product or offer for your business
- Building a new website for your project
- Preparing a presentation for a client to showcase the most impactful achievements of your collaboration
- Filming a movie with proper lighting, actors, post-production, and visual effects

In most cases, these projects require a lot of preparation, planning, and careful execution. Patience and consistency will be crucial for their success.

Fill-ins are those tedious tasks that require little effort but usually don't bring meaningful results either. Take care of them whenever you have spare time. If something better comes along, drop the fill-ins or delegate them to someone else. A few examples:

- Updating your CV with a few minor details from your latest job
- Tidying up the home screen or organizing the files on your computer
- Decluttering your desk for a more productive work environment

These are all beneficial. Still, if you have the time and energy, focusing on something from the first two categories would likely bring you better results.

Thankless tasks include various distractions, interruptions, and secondary low-impact activities. They eat up your resources and bring little to no results regarding the goal at hand, so avoid them as much as possible. Thankless tasks can vary a lot depending on the context, but here are a few examples:

- Spending hours choosing the perfect font for an already finished presentation instead of moving on to your next important objective
- Receiving a promotional email and suddenly deciding to pause all your work to unsubscribe from dozens of newsletters that you haven't read in years

The difference between fill-in and thankless tasks lies in the required effort compared to the impact that these activities will have on your primary work. For example, decluttering your desk (a fill-in task) takes relatively little time and effort, but it could create a more productive work environment with fewer distractions. On the other hand, deciding to start a deep cleanup of your whole apartment after tidying up your desk would eat up most of your time and energy for the day. Most likely, this would impair your progress on your primary work. In this context, cleaning your home is a thankless task related to your current productive goals, even though it's fairly beneficial for your general quality of life.

Of course, eliminating all your "thankless" activities isn't realistic, and delegating them may require a disproportionately large amount of time and resources. An alternative approach would be to take care of these tasks *after* your peak productivity and energy levels. For example, if you're a morning person, try focusing on your most important work in the first half of the day. Leave the tedious or unavoidable distractions for later in the evening.

Well, we just covered a whole lot of ground. Are you ready to put these ideas to work?

Action Steps

Learning about mental models and related tools is a great

start but mastering them requires intention and practice. Here are a few ideas on how to do that.

Simplify with Occam's razor. Next time you face an unclear situation or dilemma, try to identify its simplest solution. Instead of overthinking the matter, accept the explanation based on the fewest assumptions. When the situation is resolved, compare the true outcome with your projected simplest scenario. Was it far off?

Justify with Hanlon's razor. Think about the last time someone made you feel angry, undervalued, or offended. Could that person's lack of knowledge or expertise adequately explain that situation instead of wickedness?

Sure, this method has its limitations. Sometimes people may deliberately violate your rights or interests, and it would be appropriate to stand your ground and defend your values. As a rule, though, humans often make mistakes out of ignorance rather than evil intent.

Look for the satisficing solution. Next time you pick a movie to watch, a laptop to buy, or a city to visit, define just a few major criteria that have to be met. Choose the first option that aligns with these factors instead of investing too much time searching for the perfect match.

Invert your goal. Pick a recurrent task that you tend to overthink. Most likely, it would be something related to your work responsibilities. Instead of looking for ways to complete that task perfectly, start by defining the few fundamental objectives that have to be met to avoid failure.

After finishing the job, compare the results with your average performance indicators. Did you spend less time? Was this approach less stressful, with less overthinking? Are the outcomes comparable to your usual ones?

Categorize your tasks with a helpful matrix. If you keep a to-do list, try breaking down all your tasks using the Eisenhower or the Action Priority Matrix. Define the projects that need immediate attention, then plan or delegate the rest. Focus on the quick wins, avoid time-wasters and thankless tasks. Try this approach for a few days, then compare your productivity over this period with your usual experience with to-do lists.

Mental models are a fascinating topic to explore and an extremely useful skill to master for more productivity and less stress. In some situations, Occam's razor will help you simplify a complex task. In others, Hanlon's principle could save you from holding a grudge. Pareto's 80/20 rule could help you identify and focus on the vital few factors that drive the bulk of your results.

The possibilities are endless, but you have to stay patient and consistent with your practice. Every time you put these techniques to use, you'll get a little better.

But guess what?

Some mental tools and strategies can give you tremendous results and prevent a great deal of overthinking, with no practice at all. The benefits are almost instant.

In fact, the first strategy that we'll explore in the next chapter takes less than two minutes to execute.

Prepare your stopwatch.

Chapter Summary

- Mental models are concise representations of patterns, workflows, or mechanisms. They help to simplify complex processes and identify actionable steps. Examples include Pareto's principle, Occam's and Hanlon's razors, satisficing, and inversion.
- Pareto's principle states that about 80% of the consequences are driven by 20% of the causes (the vital few). The remaining 20% of the results stem from 80% of the causes (the trivial many). Whenever possible, try to invest more of your resources in the vital few activities that drive the bulk of your results.
- Occam's razor suggests that the simplest solution (with the fewest assumptions) is usually the best.
- Hanlon's razor recommends avoiding attributing to malice anything that can be adequately explained by stupidity.
- Satisficing is based on accepting the first "good enough" option instead of investing disproportionately significant resources into searching for the perfect solution.

- The inversion technique entails focusing on avoiding the negatives (failure, stupidity) instead of striving for perfection. In many scenarios, this is useful to avoid overthinking, as the factors behind failure are often more obvious and specific than abstract perfection.
- Eisenhower's Matrix and the Action Priority Matrix are useful productivity tools that have much in common with mental models. They help to categorize tasks and goals into systems depending on their urgency, importance, impact, and required effort.

6

THE 2-MINUTE RULE AND OTHER PRODUCTIVITY MIRACLES

USING SIMPLE LIFE HACKS TO TURN YOUR PROCRASTINATION INTO PROGRESS

R epetition is the key to mastery, practice makes perfect, drill leads to skill…

These principles, along with countless similar ideas, are deeply ingrained in cultures from all around the world. There's a problem, though. Repetition doesn't discriminate between beneficial and detrimental actions. Whatever is repeated is reinforced and what you water, grows.

The real trouble begins when a harmful habit is perceived as beneficial. Overthinking is one of those cases, strange as it may sound.

For example, several studies reported that people may feel that frequent worrying helps them to anticipate and prepare for upcoming potential problems. Then, because these projected dangers rarely occur, the worrying behavior is reinforced by the non-occurrence of the threats.[1]

The more often you worry, the larger the percentage of dangers that never happened, and the more this worrying behavior is reinforced. In these cases, overthinking may almost feel like a defense against the unpredictable future.

Scientists noticed a similar pattern in rumination, which is past-oriented overthinking. In many ways, it can be considered a defense mechanism, especially in people struggling with depression.

Endless rounds of rumination build a mountain of negative evidence that proves everything is hopeless. Any effort would bring no results. There's no sense in doing anything.

This false sense of certainty, albeit negative, may feel more acceptable than swinging back and forth from hope to doubt and back again. The only solution is to avoid acting altogether. This avoidance behavior reduces exposure to the seemingly adverse environment. Then, rumination is reinforced because it helps to avoid exposure to uncertainty and risk.

Here's how these misleading "benefits" of overthinking could work in an everyday scenario.

Imagine you're a freelancer writing a blog post, and you're massively overthinking the job. In your mind, you play various scenarios of how the client could criticize your work.

- What if they don't like the tone?

- What if they think the article could use more facts and sources?
- Is this paragraph too long?
- Better prepare a list of alternative headings for the sections, just in case they don't like the first set...

You go through dozens of rounds of edits before even sending over the piece for review. And then, when you finally do, the client responds with just three words.

"Great article, thanks!"

You sigh in relief and wipe off the sweat from your forehead. Mission accomplished. All that worrying and overthinking wasn't a bad thing at all. It helped you create a wonderful blog post!

But did it? Consider an alternative perspective.

The client could've given you the same feedback even if the article was considerably less sophisticated. You'll never know. What you do know is that you've overanalyzed the matter, worried about potential issues, and invested extra resources into avoiding them.

That's why there's a risk that your mind, consciously or not, could reinforce the overthinking. Simply because it "helped" to predict and avoid critique from your client. A faulty pattern is formed:

- You overthink and worry.

- You work harder to protect yourself from the threats in the future.
- All is well in the end.
- You feel the threats were avoided because you worried about them.
- Worrying and overthinking feel beneficial.
- You should keep worrying.

As a result, you get stuck in a cycle of overthinking, escaping from *potential* threats, seizing positive results, and using them as arguments in favor of your overthinking.

Of course, this level of recurrent overanalyzing can interfere with problem-solving and drastically reduce your productivity.

The time and effort you invest into crafting a brilliant article to avoid potential critique from a client could be enough to write several simpler pieces. They would still be good enough. Chances are, they'd even get an identical three-word feedback, or even a better one.

To be clear, the goal of this thesis isn't to persuade you to slack off. It wouldn't be a good idea to put little to no effort into your work and hope it will still pass off as acceptable.

So, what's the optimal approach?

Sustainable productivity without overanalyzing. In this chapter, we'll go through simple but massively effective techniques that could help you with that.

Make The Most Out Of Your Time

One thing that all types of overthinking have in common is a lack of time restrictions. Worrying about the future and ruminating over the past can take hours or days—even when the matter is not worth these investments. Too much time is wasted, and too little progress is made.

Here are a few effective ways to limit this tendency.

The Two-Minute Rule

If something useful can be done in under two minutes, do it immediately. If not, leave it for later and focus on your primary tasks. This simple filter has two major benefits.

It helps avoid "productive procrastination," when you switch to time-consuming unrelated tasks rather than focusing on what you really need to do. For example, if you're gathering the data for your quarterly report at work, doing all your laundry for the week would be productive procrastination. It takes much longer than two minutes, so leave it for later. On the other hand, freeing your desk from obvious distractors would be a fairly quick and beneficial action in the context of the primary task.

It sets boundaries for perfectionism. Overthinking can lead to countless rounds of long and exhausting reworking that often doesn't lead to any objective progress. It's like walking in place: Your legs move, but you're not going anywhere. In the book writing example, this could take the form of needlessly rewriting a given chapter over and over again. Minor edits under two minutes are fine.

Major changes? Leave them for later, after you finish the first draft of the whole book.

The only important requirement is to avoid getting lost in a long chain of quick tasks. Each of them is insignificant alone. Together, they can fuse into many lost hours if you're not careful.

The Pomodoro Technique

In the late 1980s, Francesco Cirillo developed a productivity technique based on working for short sprints of 20 to 30 minutes. As a student, he used a tomato-shaped kitchen timer to track this, hence the name *pomodoro*, "tomato" in Italian.[2]

The main goal of the technique is to reduce both external and internal distractions as much as possible. Knowing that you have to focus for just a short time reduces the resistance that you need to overcome and the likelihood of dropping the task as a result. After all, an uninterrupted three-hour work session sounds (and is) challenging. But a quick 25-minute pomodoro? Not a problem!

The original technique has six steps:

1. Choose a task to focus on.

2. Set a timer, typically for 25 minutes. This time block corresponds to one pomodoro.

3. Work on the chosen task without interruptions.

4. When the timer rings, take a short break (5 to 10 minutes).

5. Go back to step two and repeat the process until you work through four uninterrupted pomodoros.

6. After you finish the 4th pomodoro, take a longer break (20 to 30 minutes) instead of a short one.

One time block makes a pomodoro. Four pomodoros form a set. After finishing a set of pomodoros and enjoying your well-deserved long break, either pick a different task to focus on or start a new pomodoro set for your original task.

Keep in mind that pomodoros should be uninterrupted sprints of focused action. If something comes along and disturbs you in the process, you have two options:

- Abandon the pomodoro, take care of the distractor, then reset your time block. This is the preferred approach for emergencies.
- Note down and postpone the distracter. You can return to it during your break (for example, if you can finish it in under 2 minutes) or dedicate a separate pomodoro to it.

Just like the two-minute rule, the Pomodoro Technique is useful for limiting procrastination and perfectionism. Giving your mind a clear framework to follow, with focus periods and timed breaks, may help prevent it from wandering into overthinking.

Strengthen Your Attention

Modern life and work can be hectic. Often, we have to juggle several projects, keep in mind a long list of tasks, and stay in touch with multiple colleagues or clients. The main problem with all of that is that the human brain isn't good at multitasking effectively.

When you switch from one task to another, the transition is never instant and complete. This phenomenon is called *attention residue* in psychology. In a nutshell, your brain will still partially focus on task A for some time, even if you're working on task B now. As a result, your performance suffers and energy is wasted.[3]

That's why focusing on one task at a time is much better in terms of focus, overall performance, and optimization of energy resources. Instead of switching back and forth between several tasks, tackling them one by one is likely to bring you better results across the board.

A useful technique to remember in this context is the one-touch rule: Instead of saving things for later or repeatedly switching between tasks, do them as soon as you first interact with them.

For example, if you open an important email that demands your attention, answer it immediately. If you switch to another task instead, the unfinished matter will still block part of your energy and focus. This attention residue will make it harder for you to focus on the next thing until you answer that email and free your mind from it.

In the context of overthinking, attention residue can become a huge challenge. After all, the chaotic nature of worrying and rumination makes them somewhat similar to mental multitasking. Since the primary danger of any overthinking is impaired action, tasks don't get done, and the attention residue grows progressively.

Categorize Your Work

In many cases, uncertainty is at the root of overthinking. When the possibilities are endless, so are both the dangers and the potential strategies to prevent them. The mind starts overanalyzing everything in the hope of carving a certain, failproof, perfect path through life's ever-changing landscape.

Eliminating uncertainty is impossible. However, a strategy like categorization of your work could help to dial down the uncertainty and boost productivity.

Create A Tag System

One interesting approach is to tag all your tasks and projects based on a few practical factors. Then, whenever you have the opportunity to get something done, find the appropriate tags and focus on any suitable action.

Tailor your system to fit your line of work, personal traits, and available resources. Here are some ideas for tag categories:

Estimated time. Some tasks barely take a few minutes to complete (drafting a quick follow-up email), and others need several hours of focused work (writing an article). A time-based tag category could be useful when you have 10-25 available minutes but aren't sure how to use them. Instead of taking your phone to scroll through social media and kill this time, open your planner, and find the tasks tagged with [5 minutes] or [10 minutes].

Required energy. No matter how much you try, it's impossible to do high-level tasks if you're too tired or stressed. This approach is unsustainable. Instead, when you're low on energy but want to get something done, pick a task that doesn't require a lot from you. For example, this could be taking out the trash or tidying up the home screen of your computer.

Optimal tool. Much of modern work can be done on the go, but that's not always the case. For deep focus and research, you would probably prefer a laptop or PC. Drawing illustrations is much more efficient with a tablet. With a tool-based tag system, you'll always have a way to quickly check what you can do with the instruments you have at the moment.

Keep in mind that any given task could have several tags from various categories. Pick the level of sophistication for your system that would be sustainable for you both now and in the long term.

<u>Eat Your Daily Frog</u>

If you have a tiresome or unpleasant task on your plate, do it first. That's the "frog" you have to eat.

Self-development author and motivational speaker Brian Tracy popularized this technique in his best-selling book, *Eat That Frog*. Supposedly, the name of the strategy is based on a quote attributed to Mark Twain:[4]

> *If the first thing you do each morning is to eat a live frog, you can go through the day with the satisfaction of knowing that that is probably the worst thing that is going to happen to you all day long.*

The true origin of this quote is debatable.[5] However, the strategy itself is undoubtedly powerful from several perspectives.

It helps to avoid the white bear problem. If you have a tedious or challenging task on your to-do list and decide to focus on other things instead, it may keep popping up in your head the whole day. The more you try to suppress it, the more persistent it may become. By eating the frog first, you avoid the white bears later.

It reduces the attention residue you'll have stuck in your frog. Even if you don't start working on your major task, just remembering or thinking about it may be enough to lock some of your attention on it. Then, you'll have less focus available for other projects.

It makes you more likely to do the unpleasant task. Research shows that you may have a limited amount of willpower at your disposal. Activities that require self-control or self-discipline consume this resource. When you're out of it, you may find it harder to stay disciplined. This psychological phenomenon is called ego depletion.[6] In other words, it's much easier to do an unpleasant task earlier in the day, before you use up most of your willpower on other tasks.

Besides the matter of productivity, eating your daily frog as soon as possible may benefit your mood. It's way easier to enjoy your day knowing that its most unpleasant part is over.

Before we move on to other exciting topics, here's a quick reminder.

You don't need to use all strategies and tips from the last few chapters at the same time. Just like physical tools, mental models and thought techniques have different applications.

In some cases, you would get better results from using the Eisenhower Matrix, maybe coupled with a tag system, to categorize your tasks. Other times, just eating your frog first thing in the morning would be enough. For sessions of deep work, try the Pomodoro Technique. When you're pressed for time, keep in mind the two-minute rule and the one-touch principle.

Action Steps

Enjoy some Italian tomatoes for deep work. Pomodoros, more specifically. Pick a task or project to focus on, eliminate as many distractions as possible, and set your timer for 25 minutes. After finishing your first pomodoro, take a five-minute break and start the next one. Later, after your fourth pomodoro, check your progress. How would you rate your productivity? Was it easier to focus in such short sprints of work?

Tag the tasks on your to-do list. This approach is easier to test with a productivity app of your choice, as most of them offer the option to add tags to your action items. Alternatively, you could tag the tasks in a physical to-do list by marking each point with a distinct color. For example, use a green dot to mark quick tasks that can be finished in under five minutes, a yellow one for somewhat longer tasks, or a red dot for complex projects that require a whole lot of time, focus, and energy. After some time, evaluate if this approach makes it easier for you to navigate your to-do list and pick the right task when needed.

Eat your frog. Most people tend to postpone unpleasant or challenging tasks, losing a lot of time and energy in the process. Next time you feel like following this pattern, do the opposite. Identify your frog and take care of it first thing in the morning. At the end of the day, analyze your overall mood, energy levels, and productivity. Do you feel the effects of dealing with your biggest challenge before the less troublesome tasks?

All these strategies can give you an almost instant boost in focus and productivity but mastering them still takes dedication.

The more you practice these approaches, the better you'll get at using them.

Recurrent overthinking reinforces this habit, but the same principle works for mental models, thought strategies, and productivity techniques. You get what you repeat.

That's just how the human brain works. It's a wonderful machine, but it has its laws and limitations. To help overcome some of them, it may be a good idea to get yourself an extra brain.

In the next chapter, we'll explore how to do just that.

Chapter Summary

- People may feel as if their overthinking is helpful. For example, worrying can be perceived as protection from threats in the future.
- In reality, any overthinking may impair action or make it highly inefficient. Recurrent overanalyzing interferes with productive action and focuses more on the problem instead of the solution.
- Some techniques that may help against overanalyzing include time management, attention support, and task categorization.
- If a useful task takes less than two minutes, consider doing it immediately instead of postponing it. (The two-minute rule.)

- For deep work, the Pomodoro Technique could be useful. It consists of short 25-minute periods of focused work without distractions (pomodoros), followed by short 5-10-minute breaks.
- Whenever possible, avoid multitasking to avoid impairing attention and wasting energy.
- Instead of switching tasks or saving them for later, a helpful approach may be to work on them immediately after you first interact with them. (The one-touch rule.)
- Try categorizing your tasks with a tag system for faster and easier access in different scenarios.
- Whenever possible, deal with your most unpleasant or challenging tasks before moving on to the less demanding ones.

7

IS YOUR BRAIN AT FULL CAPACITY?

EXPLORE THE POWER OF THESE 3 PROVEN EXTERNAL BRAIN SYSTEMS AND FIND THE PERFECT FIT FOR YOU

How many things can you keep in mind at the same time?

For over half a century already, neuroscientists and psychologists have believed that the human brain can hold, on average, only a limited number of objects in its short-term memory. This concept is sometimes called Miller's law, named after the cognitive psychologist George A. Miller.

In 1956, Miller published a fascinating study on the capacity of short-term memory in humans.[1] According to this paper, the average brain can effectively hold and retrieve about seven (plus or minus two) objects. These could be letters, numbers, words, or other "chunks" of information.

A single chunk is the largest meaningful unit of information that a person recognizes in a given set of data, depending on their background, skills, and other individual factors.

For example, you won't have much trouble memorizing a list of seven words in your native language. Each corresponds to one chunk of meaningful information, describing a single object or concept. That makes them relatively easy to process, memorize, and retrieve.

On the other hand, if you had to memorize a list of seven words in an unfamiliar foreign language, your brain would split each into recognizable chunks of familiar syllables or sounds. As a result, it would be exceedingly hard to memorize all seven foreign words without using any special techniques, as they would make much more than seven chunks of information to you.

With focused training and different mnemonic techniques, you could expand your short-term memory capacity. However, the general principle stands: The human brain isn't effective in keeping a lot of things in mind.

Ironically, that's precisely the challenge that modern times put before us.

Life in the 21st century can be quite hectic in terms of information. From dusk till dawn our brains are bombarded with various stimuli, news, advertisements, work-related tasks, messages from friends and family, unexpected ideas, and sudden cravings. Most of these are meaningful only short-term.

Even within a single domain like your work, the overabundance of short-term information can quickly lead to mental clutter. In turn, this can impair attention and decision-making. This happens partly due to the attention residue phenomenon that we explored in the previous chapter, and partly due to the analysis paralysis that may set in when you face a lot of options.

So how can we navigate the barrage of short-term information if the human brain is limited to 7 ± 2 objects on average?

Many solutions have been proposed over the last decades. Collectively, most of them are often referred to as "external brain systems."

Two Minds Are Better Than One

An external brain system is an unofficial collective term for different approaches to organizing tasks, ideas, and reference materials for future use.

The human brain can't keep up with the breakneck speed of technological progress. The relentless influx of information that we face through modern communication channels goes well beyond the seven chunks we can process and retrieve effectively without external tools.

Within a single day, you could get:

- Dozens of work-related tasks, shared with you via email or a messaging app like Slack

- At least a couple of marketing announcements from brands that you trust and follow
- Several book recommendations for your field of professional or personal interest either as a tip from someone or from social media
- Multiple check-ins and questions from family and friends
- Incidental "Aha!" moments and bright ideas that you could pursue later

To successfully navigate the era of information, an elegant solution would be to have an extra mind to categorize and store all the incoming information. An external brain, if you will. One that better fits the modern reality and can store much more than a few chunks of information.

The difference between this external brain system and a simple list of tasks lies in how information is categorized and stored. A single list would quickly grow out of control after a few days or weeks due to the number of items in it.

Besides being an effective way to declutter the mind from informational noise, having an external brain system could also help your primary brain get a well-deserved rest. After all, keeping all your thoughts and tasks in mind and worrying about forgetting or missing any of them is exhausting.

When you know that all that information is safely stored in a well-organized system, you can finally relax. With this peace of mind, you'll have more mental resources to focus on the project and then return to your other projects whenever the time is right.

Your primary brain takes care of your creative, focused, meaningful work. Your "external" brain takes care of storing the information for future use.

So, what can this external brain look like?

Below, we'll explore some of the most interesting options that emerged over the last decades.

If any of these overviews resonates with you, make sure to dive deeper into the original concept to study it. Each of these strategies comes from a fabulous book and has its own vibrant community of adepts that share ideas and tips on how to further master the system.

The Getting Things Done (Gtd) System By David Allen

In his eponymous book, productivity consultant David Allen described a system he called *Getting Things Done* (GTD).[2]

The core mechanism behind this approach is crystallized in Allen's words:

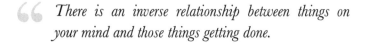 *There is an inverse relationship between things on your mind and those things getting done.*

So, to get more things done, get them off your mind!

The GTD system is based on a workflow that helps to free the mind from the burden of storing and controlling incoming tasks. How? Primarily by documenting them elsewhere or taking care of them immediately.

The whole process consists of five stages: capture, clarify, organize, reflect, and engage.

Stage 1: Capture. All your tasks, ideas, documents, and other objects are captured in a single *Inbox* destination. This could be a note-taking app, a text file on your device of choice, or anything similar. The important part here is to note down or otherwise document the incoming information, freeing your mind from the necessity of storing it on its own.

Stages 2: Clarify. Analyze the incoming information by answering the following five questions:

- Is this item actionable?
- Can it be completed in a single step?
- Does it take more than two minutes?
- Is this your responsibility?
- Does it have a specific day or time of completion?

Stage 3: Organize. Depending on your answers to the questions in the first step, all the tasks and ideas from your inbox will end up in one of the possible destinations.

1. Trash: non-actionable items, useless information. For example, an advertisement from your favorite brand, but the sales offer has expired.

2. Reference archive: non-actionable items or information that could be useful later. This includes books, journals, cheat sheets, guidelines, reports, and similar documents.
3. Immediate action list: short single-step tasks that can be completed in less than two minutes. If this task is not your direct responsibility, delegate it to someone.
4. Plans: multi-step items and complex projects that require planning. This could be writing a report for work, learning a new skill, putting up a website, or renovating a room in your house. Plan these tasks in detail in the next stage of the process (Stage 4: Reflect).
5. Scheduled tasks in your calendar: relatively simple and short tasks that have a specific day or time of completion. For example, sending a follow-up email to your coworker, visiting your dentist for a regular checkup, or going to the gym.

Stage 4: Reflect. For multi-step tasks that take a significant time, additional planning is required. Reflect on how you could break these big projects into smaller ones. If needed, check your reference archive for assistance, delegate part of the workflow, or schedule specific tasks for a specific day and time later.

Stage 5: Engage. Even the most meticulous organizing and planning is useless without action. After bringing order to your GTD system, start taking care of the appropriate tasks.

- Finish the short tasks that take less than two minutes
- Check your calendar for specific actions today
- Start working on the next steps in your complex projects

Allen recommends emptying your inbox of tasks daily or weekly. In other words, processing all the entries in your inbox and moving them to their most suitable destinations (e.g., calendar, archive, trash). This approach helps to keep your short-term memory free from mental clutter.

Every task that's worth scheduling will be waiting in your calendar. Complex projects will be broken down into smaller steps and planned ahead. Quick and easy tasks will be finished immediately or delegated to someone.

No need to memorize anything! All your most important tasks, projects and ideas will be neatly categorized in your external brain, the GTD system.

The Bullet Journal System By Ryder Carroll

In 2013, digital product designer Ryder Carroll published his Bullet Journal system online.[3] Sometimes abbreviated to just BuJo, this approach has become extremely popular over the following years.

The name "bullet journal" comes from the term "bullet points," meaning components of an unnumbered list.

Most of the information in Carroll's system is stored and organized in this format. Additionally, the name references the preferred use of dot journals instead of lined ones.

Bullet journals are usually physical, handwritten in a single notebook of your choice. Let's go through the essential components of the system.

The index is usually located at the beginning of the journal. Like a table of contents in a book, the index of your BuJo helps you find a specific project or period in your notebook.

The key is a short explanation of common symbols used in your lists. For example, you could use a simple dot (•) for tasks, a circle (○) for events, and a dash (–) for notes. Sometimes a cross (x) is used to mark completed items and an arrow (>) for postponed tasks. Make sure to customize the level of sophistication of your BuJo key to fit your personal preferences.

Logs are simplified overviews of specific periods. Use daily, weekly, and monthly logs to keep track of your projects, goals, deadlines, and their related projects.

For example, here's what a quick monthly log could look like:

On the left page, the owner of this journal included a stylized overview of the month in a single block. This could be useful for marking important upcoming dates or just getting a general overview of the month.

On the right page, the same month is logged as a column with dates and their corresponding days of the week (in this case, in Dutch). On both sides of the column, there's some space for notes, reminders, or tasks.

Collections organize your information by type of content. These could be lists, progress bars, or consistency trackers, depending on your goals and lifestyle. Here are some examples:

- A *list of books* that you've already read or plan to read this year.

- A *habit tracker* to make sure you're going for a run at least twice a week.
- A *progress bar* that you gradually "fill up" as you save or invest money toward a goal.
- A *collection of quotes* that resonate with you and keep you inspired.
- A *mood archive of the year*, in which you would draw a small square of a particular color to represent your average mood that day to keep track of your mental health in the long term. For example, a blue square for when you're feeling sad, a red one for angry days, or a green one for happy times.

Collections usually make the bulk of a bullet journal.

The GTD system and the BuJo approach have a fundamental thing in common: They are designed to free as much of your "mental bandwidth" as possible. Instead of keeping tasks and ideas in the back of your mind, you add them to your inbox (GTD) or a suitable log or collection (BuJo).

The Second Brain System By Tiago Forte

 *Our brains are for having ideas, not storing them.*[4]

This is the core idea behind the Second Brain system, developed by author and productivity coach Tiago Forte. In his best-selling book *Building a Second Brain*, Forte describes the process of creating a digital repository for your ideas, inspiration, and any kind of useful information.

Similar to Allen's GTD system, the Second Brain is based on a simple algorithm for processing incoming data: the CODE method (capture, organize, distill, express).

Capture

During the capture stage, the goal is to document all the information that feels interesting, valuable, or useful. Use any tool that feels the most comfortable. It could be a physical notebook, a note-taking app on your smartphone, a Notion or Obsidian database, or even a voice recording.

Organize

Every once in a while, organize the incoming information using the PARA method (projects, areas, resources, archive) according to its actionability. Here's a list of its components ranging from most actionable to least actionable.

Projects are short-term tasks (professional or personal) that you take on with a specific goal in mind. These are all the things that you're working on right now (or will in the near future), for example:

- An idea for your next blog post
- A recipe for tomorrow's lunch
- A few notes on choosing and buying a new computer

Areas of responsibility include critical aspects of your work or life that you want to manage consistently over time. For example:

- Professional: productivity, time management, marketing, design
- Personal: health, physical activity, hobbies, home

Resources contain your topics of interest, everything that feels exciting to learn and explore. Depending on your lifestyle and personal preferences, these could be related to:

- Your favorite genre of movies or books
- Meditation
- Creative writing
- Dog training

In other words, a resource would be anything and everything unrelated to a specific project or area but still enriches your life.

Finally, your **Archive** would contain anything from the previous three categories that are no longer important or active.

- Finished tasks and projects
- Areas of responsibility that are no longer relevant
- Resources that you are not interested in anymore

Distill

An essential part of keeping your "second brain" well-organized and easy to navigate is to distill all your entries into actionable, bite-sized notes.

For example, instead of writing a 10-page summary of a documentary that you just finished watching, note down just a few salient points. Instead of saving a full transcription of a three-hour meeting, capture just the actionable steps and make sure to address them.

This process of crystallizing the information in your system makes it so much easier to discover unexpected connections between different topics, ideas, and resources. In turn, this makes every bit of information much more actionable and useful.

Express

In his Second Brain system, Tiago Forte emphasizes the importance of using your information and ideas to achieve tangible results in the real world.

The goal isn't just to use the Second Brain as a well-organized information warehouse. Instead, it can be a factory where you would process that information into something useful and beautiful for the world. Collections of facts on a specific topic can be turned into infographics. Your notes from meetings at work could become the base for Q&A documents or even company guidelines.

This focus on the actionability of stored information is common in all versions of external brain systems. GTD, the Bullet Journal, and the Second Brain are designed to streamline the process of storing information, organizing it in a well-defined system, and then putting it to good use.

So far, we've focused mostly on the benefits of setting up an external brain system. Let's take a moment to consider the potential challenges and issues, too.

Double The Brains, Not The Headache

No matter what external brain strategy you choose, it's crucial to keep in mind that it's just a tool. And like any tool, it will have limitations, requirements, and drawbacks.

Find What Works For You

There's no one-size-fits-all approach to building a second brain system. The framework that's comfortable and helpful for some people will feel like a major burden to others. You'll have to try different frameworks to find the one that's truly yours, then personalize it even further.

For example, the *Bullet Journal* system usually works better for people who enjoy writing and doodling in physical notebooks. They may feel as if there's something almost therapeutic in putting pen to paper without the intrusive light of a gadget's screen.

Other people may see notebooks as impractical and outdated. They feel more comfortable setting up a *GTD* system in their smartphone's app. Most offer additional features, like adding tags to your tasks and entries or using a search bar to find whatever you're looking for in mere seconds.

The *Second Brain* approach is much more flexible and simpler than the first two options. Some people like this simplicity. Others might feel it's way too abstract and it could use a few more destinations besides the four PARA categories (projects, areas, resources, archive).

Keep Your System Tidy

All external brain systems have to be maintained in order. GTD, BuJo, and the Second Brain—all of them are based on regular reviews of your "inbox" of captured information. Otherwise, everything goes out of control, leaving you with a bloated list that's tough to navigate and use.

Just like your first brain has a specific place and application for every piece of information, your external brain should safely store your tasks, ideas, projects, and references in different categories. You'll get the most out of this system only if you keep it tidy.

Make Your Framework Serve You (Not The Other Way Around)

The common goals of all external brain systems are:

- Decluttering your brain from all the informational noise that thins out your focus
- Helping your brain to relax and temporarily disconnect from your tasks, knowing that they're safely stored for when you'll be ready
- Bringing more order to your creative endeavors, work projects, and personal interests

However, there's a risk of going overboard with your system's levels of sophistication and complexity. Ideally, it should be easy to maintain without investing too much time into it. After all, your system is meant to serve YOU, not force you to serve IT.

Action Steps

Start building your second mind. Hopefully, now you have a general idea of how an external brain system could look and work. Now, it's time to test it out. Out of the three external brain systems that we touched upon in this chapter, pick the one that resonates with you for any reason. Use it for at least one week, then evaluate your progress. Does this system help you reduce mental clutter? Are you overthinking less frequently?

If needed, explore the nuances of this system by picking up the author's original book. Here's a quick list:

- David Allen, *Getting Things Done: The Art of Stress-Free Productivity*[2]

- Ryder Carroll, *The Bullet Journal Method: Track the Past, Order the Present, Design the Future*[5]
- Tiago Forte, *Building a Second Brain: A Proven Method to Organise Your Digital Life and Unlock Your Creative Potential*[6]

Give your brain a well-deserved rest. This week, instead of burdening your primary brain, deposit all your tasks and ideas into your chosen second brain. Later, circle back to this information and organize it appropriately.

One of the most useful and powerful benefits of any external brain system is that it gives you a space to quickly store all ideas, tasks, projects, and resources you may need later. It's way more comfortable and effective than trying to remember everything on your own.

Here's a quick example. Imagine you go to the grocery store without a bag or cart. You'll manage to carry a bottle of milk on your own. What's the big deal? Well...

Ten minutes in, you're balancing a towering pile of products in your arms. It's uncomfortable, mildly stressful, and comes with the added risk of breaking a few eggs. Carrying your items in a shopping cart would've been more effective and comfortable. The same goes for keeping your tasks and ideas in a suitable framework.

With a working external storage system for your information, the limited short-term memory of the human brain isn't a problem anymore. With less clutter, lower stress, and a better-organized life, making decisions and taking action should get much easier. Terrific job!

Now, let's bring this up a notch. To get the most out of your decisions and actions, you have to align them with your goals.

Think about your external brain system as a map. It helps you navigate a vast ocean of information more effectively and with less stress. But where do you want to sail in the first place? How do you find the right direction?

Having just a map won't be enough for this.

You need a compass. Deceivingly simple, this instrument can make all the difference between a successful voyage and a shipwreck.

In the next chapter, we'll get familiar with the most powerful compass for less overthinking and more productivity: the art of setting effective goals.

Chapter Summary

- The human brain is excellent at processing and synthesizing new ideas but it has a limited capacity for storing short-term information.
- There's an overabundance of short-term information in modern life and work. Trying to retain it on your own is counterproductive and stressful.

- One possible solution to this limitation is setting up an "external brain system" to organize and store all the information that's interesting or useful to you.
- Some examples of external brain systems include the Getting Things Done (GTD) system by David Allen, the Bullet Journal (BuJo) method by Ryder Carroll, and the Second Brain system by Tiago Forte.
- All external brain systems have a few common traits: They emphasize the importance of quick and easy capture of information, require regular reviews and tidying up, and promote action instead of just hoarding data.

8

SMART VS. PACT

FIND OUT WHICH GOAL-SETTING HELPS YOU GET WHERE YOU SEE YOURSELF IN 3, 5, OR 10 YEARS

I magine you have a fully equipped ship ready to embark on a treasure hunt. It's perfectly functional, stocked up on provision, and staffed by a well-trained crew. Its navigation maps are the most accurate and detailed that money can buy. In other words, everything is ready for action. Your vessel seems destined for great adventures, discoveries, and glory.

The only problem? You're not sailing anywhere.

You may have a vague idea of where the treasure is hidden. Or it may be specific enough to see it on your state-of-the-art map, but you're still figuring out the details of the path.

Months pass by, and your glorious ship is still anchored in the local port. The treasure is still buried on the other side of the world. You're still overthinking the details.

But what if you place less emphasis on the *treasure* and more on your *compass*?

James Clear, author of the best-selling book *Atomic Habits*, puts this beautifully:[1]

> *Your goal becomes your compass, not your buried treasure. The goal is your direction, not your destination. The goal is a mission that you are on, a path that you follow.*

The strategies and systems from the previous chapters are more than helpful for preparing your ship.

- Overall, your external brain system is similar to a map where you add all potential routes, destinations, potential dangers, and hidden treasures.
- The archive of valuable resources in your external brain is like a storage compartment full of provisions and equipment.
- The mental models you've mastered are like drills and training for the crew, helping them to solve common issues more effectively.

But without actually setting sail and slowly progressing toward the treasure, all of the above makes little sense. It doesn't serve its purpose. That's the main danger of overthinking: It becomes unhealthy when it leads to indecision and inaction. Often, this isn't necessarily a fault of your system, skills, or knowledge. They're just tools, after all.

In many cases, poorly formulated goals may promote overthinking and impair progress.

In the example above, the treasure itself can't be a compelling goal. It's a result, a benefit, a prize. The goal, on the other hand, is to *reach* the treasure. To sail out, navigate the ocean, reach the destination, find the spot, dig up the rusty chest, and then (finally!) enjoy the gold inside.

By focusing on the process—the compass, the journey—it's much easier to make consistent progress. In this chapter, we'll go through specific strategies for setting goals that reduce overthinking and propel your progress.

Envision The Details

Abstract concepts and goals are hardly actionable. Besides phrasing your plans in specific terms, another good technique is to imagine yourself sitting down and starting the work. What will you do first? What comes after that?

In his book *Smarter Faster Better*, journalist and author Charles Duhigg puts it this way:[2]

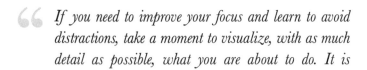

> *If you need to improve your focus and learn to avoid distractions, take a moment to visualize, with as much detail as possible, what you are about to do. It is*

easier to know what's ahead when there's a well-rounded script inside your head.

Then, whenever something outside of this mental script pops up, it's easier to notice that it doesn't belong in the picture instead of falling into the distraction.

If you need to present a report at work, how would you prepare the slideshow?

Imagine yourself opening PowerPoint, Google Slides, Keynote, or another presentation program on your computer. Imagine drafting the first slide, with a simple title. A few slides for the content, maybe with several diagrams. One final screen for the conclusion. After the draft is finished, you'll choose the font and tweak the transitions. If needed, send the finished file to a coworker for discussion.

This imaginary plan isn't too detailed, but it still gives you a good idea of the path ahead. No detours to do the laundry, mop the floors, or cook lasagna.

Follow the path you've envisioned.

Focus On The Immediate Next Action

Every outstanding achievement is the result of hundreds or thousands of tiny steps. Focusing on the immediate next action is easier and less intimidating than thinking too much about the whole path ahead.

Instead of dreaming about the treasure, you focus just on the next step in the direction that your compass suggests.

Instead of fantasizing about your dream physique, you take care of today's workout at the gym with everything you've got.

For complex multi-step tasks, split them into 20 (or as many as you need) tiny little steps. Take care of them one by one. This way, a vague and terrifying "relocate to Germany" turns into:

1. Go to the vet and check if the cat's passport and vaccines meet the requirements for entering Germany.
2. Find an apartment for rent online.
3. Call the landlord and arrange the details.
4. Order a dozen cardboard boxes for packing.
5. Sort books. Decide which ones to take and which to sell or donate.

And so on, for as many steps as needed. Simple bite-sized tasks are easier to process and complete. By focusing on them one by one, you'll get through the whole journey much more effectively, with less stress and overthinking.

By breaking down major projects into smaller steps, you'll also lower the perceived level of difficulty of the work ahead.

Why is this important?

According to some studies, there's an inverted U-shaped correlation between task difficulty and applied effort.[3] Researchers noticed the lowest level of performance in tasks that were too easy or too challenging.

At the same time, more recent research by Locke and colleagues revealed a linear correlation between goal difficulty and effort.[4] The more challenging the goal (within realistic limits and personal ability), the higher the performance.

That's why it's crucial to set meaningful and challenging goals but break them down into tasks that don't feel too difficult on their own. The second part of the equation is where most people fall short. As a result, they find themselves stuck with way too ambitious and overwhelming goals without actionable components. Little to no progress is made, and the whole project is dropped.

Apply The Pact Method

There's a high chance that you've heard about the SMART approach to goal-setting. It's an acronym that states that effective goals should be _S_pecific, _M_easurable, _A_ttainable, _R_ealistic, and _T_ime-bound.

One of its downsides, though, is that it doesn't put much emphasis on how meaningful or consistent the goal in question is. As a result, it works best for those bite-sized components of major projects.

At the same time, the SMART approach puts a heavy focus on the desired outcome of the work. By definition, it needs Specific, Measurable, and Time-bound goals, which limits the magnitude of the project. Ambitious work may feel too overwhelming when adorned with too many numbers.

In the context of meaningful, ambitious, long-term goals, a better approach might be the PACT method, proposed by neuroscientist and writer Anne-Laure Le Cunff.[5] It stands for _P_urposeful, _A_ctionable, _C_ontinuous, and _T_rackable.

- Purposeful: Your goals should feel meaningful to you long-term, not just right now. It's aligned with your core values, dreams, and aspirations.
- Actionable: Your progress toward this goal should be based on an output that's within your immediate control.
- Continuous: The efforts toward this goal should be regular and consistent. It's not a single-time task but a long-term journey toward something great.
- Trackable: You should be able to track whether or not you're taking the action needed to progress on your path. The magnitude of this progress is secondary.

Both the SMART and the PACT approach have their benefits and drawbacks. In different situations, you may prefer one over the other.

To Smart Or To Pact? That Is The Question

Let's circle back to the treasure hunt analogy from the beginning of the chapter. How could this goal be set using the SMART and the PACT method for comparison?

SMART: Dig up the treasure chest that's hidden on Island X within the next 90 days.

PACT: Sail for at least five hours every day toward Island X to dig up the treasure hidden there.

The difference is subtle but essential. SMART focuses on the treasure; PACT emphasizes the journey. Here are a few other examples:

SMART:

- Get 5,000 followers on my brand's Instagram page this year by posting more Reels.
- Lose seven pounds of body fat in the next two months through dieting and exercise.
- Find two new clients for my advertising agency this week with the help of cold outreach.

PACT:

- Post one new Reel to my brand's Instagram page to attract new followers for my brand.
- Go to the gym every other day and avoid sweetened soft drinks to eventually drop some weight and feel comfortable in my favorite pair of jeans.

- Send five cold emails to potential new clients every day until I seize two new projects for my advertising agency.

The PACT method is extremely effective at curbing overthinking tendencies for several reasons.

First, it doesn't require any planning at all. You just pick a meaningful goal, define the continuous actions that would move you forward, and then start walking.

SMART goals, on the other hand, need considerably more planning to be effective. After all, you'll be dealing with time boundaries and measurable outcomes. This comes with a risk of overanalyzing the plan too much, which could impair decision-making and consistent action.

Second, the PACT method gives you more agency, as it focuses on your output. As long as you do the required actions and track them consistently, you're making progress. Your ship is sailing forward, and the treasure slowly approaches. For example, you're posting one Reel on your Instagram page to attract new followers.

With SMART goals, your actions are still important but the spotlight is on the result. As such, there's a higher risk of external forces affecting the project's success. After all, you can post one Reel daily but you can't directly make people subscribe to your page. That's out of your direct control, and yet that's the emphasis of your SMART goal.

Last but not least, PACT goals give you much more space to reassess your focus (actions) along the journey. If you're posting one Reel per day, you can experiment with different formats, publication times, captions, hashtags, etc. As long as you're doing the work, you're on the right path.

In SMART goals, the focus (result) is set in stone. Changing it halfway through the process would feel like cheating. Or like failure.

"Dig up the ~~treasure chest~~ rusty horseshoe that's hidden on Island X within the next 90 days."

"Get ~~5,000~~ 5 followers on my brand's Instagram page this year by posting more Reels."

Remember the growth mindset concept that we explored in Chapter 4? The one that focuses more on effort and the possibility of gradual improvement (e.g. studying) rather than achieving specific results (e.g. passing a test)? In many ways, that's the difference between the PACT and the SMART method.

However, this dynamic doesn't mean that one strategy is intrinsically better than the other. Everything depends on the situation, the task, and your personal preferences.

The SMART approach usually works better with onetime and relatively simple tasks. For example, *"Send a 100-word follow-up email to Bob regarding our planned trip."* The PACT method is more suitable for long-term, complex goals that require consistent progress. *"Send a short daily email to my brand's subscribers to keep them engaged."*

Some people are more productive with measurable goals and specific time limits. Others tend to overthink less when they focus on the continuous everyday steps instead of the results.

Just like with all the other approaches and strategies we've explored so far, there's no universal solution. Be ready to experiment and mix different tactics depending on the situation.

Jab, Cross, Left Hook… KO!

Each of the techniques and strategies that we've covered so far in this book can be effective on their own. Mental models, priority matrices, external brain systems, goal-setting methods… All these help to reduce overthinking and boost productivity.

However, if you want to supercharge your progress, learn to use these tools together. Just like a boxer throws fluid combinations of jabs, hooks, and uppercuts to knock out their opponent.

Here's how it could look in practice:

1. Set up an *external brain system* to keep everything organized. Keep your tasks, projects, and reference materials in separate destinations.

2. Using the *Eisenhower Matrix,* categorize your tasks by urgency and importance.

3. Take care of the emergencies (urgent, important) by setting *SMART short-term goals,* e.g. *"Find 5 potential venues (within our budget) for the meeting of stakeholders scheduled for next week."*

4. After dealing with the emergencies, see if there are any trivial and low-level things that you can quickly eliminate using *the two-minute rule.* Great, now you've freed a good part of your mind to take on more meaningful projects!

5. Using the *PACT method,* define your most important long-term goals and their projects. Start making meaningful progress toward them with daily actions.

6. To define which activities could make the most impact, remember the *80/20 principle.* What 20% of tasks or actions would bring you 80% of your desired results?

Of course, these are all just suggestions. You can make your approach as sophisticated (or simple) as you want. As long as it helps you overthink less and act more, it's perfectly valid.

Action Steps

Visualize your future work. Next time you find yourself procrastinating or overanalyzing, try to sit down and imagine how you will work on the task at hand. What tools will you use? What reference materials will you pick from your archive? Envision the path you'll take to complete this project. See if this makes it easier to get started and avoid any distractions on the way.

Divide and conquer. Think about your biggest or most complex project right now. Break it down into 10 to 20 smaller steps. Try to complete at least three of them this week. Do you feel less of a resistance when you approach your project this way?

Make an imPACT. Test this strategy by picking one major goal and crystallizing it with the PACT method. Set a long-term destination and start moving, without a complex plan or too many restrictions. Consistency beats intensity. Making tiny steps day after day for a whole year in the chosen direction will get you miles farther than you think.

SMART vs. PACT. One interesting experiment could be taking a previous SMART goal that you didn't accomplish and reformatting it into a PACT version. See if this new approach helps you make more progress. Do you overthink less when you focus on the process instead of the destination?

In this chapter, we explored several perspectives on goal-setting. Remember, however, that even the most effective systems and the best-designed goals aren't immune to unexpected events, mistakes, and imperfections overall.

It's all a natural part of life. Instead of feverishly striving for perfection in everything, it's important to find opportunities and beauty even in incidental failures.

With the right mindset and a bit of dedication, a broken item can turn from a pile of rubbish into a work of art. In the East, this principle has been known for many centuries.

For our last chapter, I invite you to join me on an imaginary trip to the Land of the Rising Sun.

There, imperfection gave birth to one of the most beautiful forms of traditional craftsmanship.

A celebration of flaws in porcelain and gold.

Chapter Summary

- One of the biggest complications of overthinking is impaired action. This thwarted progress may be caused by the absence of a clear or inspiring goal.
- Most people tend to put the least effort into *tasks* that are too easy or too hard. At the same time, the more challenging a *goal* feels, the more effort we are usually willing to put into achieving it. To make use of these two principles, a good approach is to pick quite challenging and inspiring goals but break them down into smaller, less intimidating tasks.
- The PACT method recommends setting goals that are Purposeful, Actionable, Continuous, and Trackable. This strategy emphasizes taking

action consistently, no matter how small, instead of focusing too much on the destination.

- The classic SMART method suggests setting goals that are Specific, Measurable, Attainable, Realistic, and Time-bound. It doesn't clarify specific steps or actions, focusing mostly on the result.

- Both approaches have their own strengths and weaknesses. SMART goals are usually more suitable for relatively simpler and short-term projects. PACT goals may work better with long-term and more meaningful goals.

- Combining various mental models, productivity tips, and task organization systems may improve their overall effectiveness.

9

READY TO TRANSCEND THE ERA OF PERFECTIONISM?

BREAK THE HABIT OF OVERTHINKING ONCE AND FOR ALL SO YOU CAN FOCUS ON THE MORE IMPORTANT ASPECTS OF LIFE

One day, shogun Ashikaga Yoshimasa shattered his favorite tea bowl.

The mighty warlord sent the item to China for repairs. Weeks passed, then some more. The tea bowl finally returned. Once elegant and beautiful, now it was riddled with unsightly metal staples holding the fragments together!

The shogun's dismay knew no boundaries. Yoshimasa ordered local Japanese craftsmen to develop a new, visually pleasant method for repairing broken ceramics. According to the legend, that's how the art of *kintsugi* was born sometime in the late 15th century.[1]

Kintsugi or *kintsukuroi* means "golden joinery" or "golden repair," respectively. This technique mends broken ceramics with a mixture of lacquer with gold, silver, or platinum powder. Here's how the result can look:

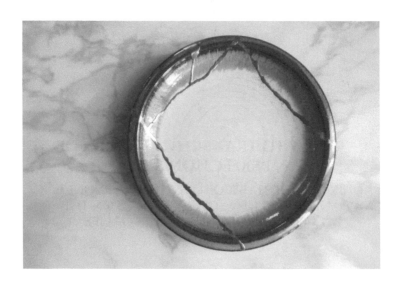

Besides being an aesthetically pleasant form of pottery repair, kintsugi is also one of the best embodiments of the Japanese *wabi-sabi* philosophy. Hardly translatable into accurate English terms, wabi represents beauty in simplicity, while sabi is an appreciation for the used, old, and rusty.

Embracing wabi-sabi means finding beauty in imperfection, transience, and incompleteness. Every object and being has a life full of highs and lows, victories and wounds. The scars we gather on the way are part of our unique history. Instead of hiding or disguising them, we can find beauty in their forms—golden mends on your favorite tea bowl.

In many ways, wabi-sabi is a healthy alternative and a practical solution to overthinking induced by perfectionism.

More Options Than Atoms In The Universe

As we explored in previous chapters, overthinking is often based on an underlying fear of failure. This may lead to striving for perfection as the ultimate guarantee against catastrophe. The *ideal* business won't go bankrupt. A *flawless* song will avoid harsh criticism. The *perfect* chess opening will prevent you from losing the game.

The problem with this approach is that perfection is a vague concept, largely subjective, and vulnerable to external forces. These three factors raise the stakes and intensify anxiety, forcing one to prepare for an ever-increasing number of variables. Then, the more options and choices are considered, the worse the overthinking gets.

Take chess as a straightforward and calculable example. You must choose from "just" 20 opening moves on your first turn. After three moves from each player, the number of possible positions on the chessboard is already at a staggering 119,060,324 variants. From there, the numbers get even more immense with every turn.

Mathematicians calculated that the overall number of legal chess moves and positions could be between 10^{44} and 10^{123}. In other words, there may exist more possible chess games than atoms in the observable universe, estimated to be around 10^{80}.[2]

And that's just chess. Domains like music, writing, business, and even human relationships likely have a greater number of possible outcomes after every action. Millions of possible options exist for a first stroke of the paintbrush on a blank canvas. Which is the perfect one? To an overthinker, this might feel terrifying.

Concepts like the Japanese wabi-sabi offer a whole different perspective on life and work. Instead of succumbing to fear of failure and accepting perfectionism as an unrealistic form of protection against it, a wiser approach may be learning to appreciate the fleeting nature of all things.

In his book *Wabi Sabi Simple*, Richard Powell explains this mindset in the following terms:[3]

> *Wabi-sabi nurtures all that is authentic by acknowledging three simple realities: nothing lasts, nothing is finished, and nothing is perfect.*

If these principles sound overly pessimistic, imagine an oak tree in the forest. It may be hundreds of years old, but it most definitely won't live forever. It will never be quite finished or complete, always growing while it's alive and providing nourishment to other life-forms after its death. It will never be perfect, as there is no ideal standard. And yet this oak tree is majestic nonetheless, with a unique story that will never be repeated. Appreciating this beauty is the remedy to impermanence, incompleteness, and imperfection.

The same train of thought applies to any kind of work, art, or personal achievement. Nothing lasts, nothing is finished, nothing is perfect—mostly because it's impossible to achieve any of those. Instead of chasing the impossible, it would be better to appreciate reality and adapt to it. From a broken tea bowl to an oak tree to your current project at work, the principle stands.

But why is perfectionism so common, especially in modern times?

The Perfectionism Pandemic

In 2019, the American Psychological Association published a meta-analysis on the generational change in perfectionism levels among college students.[4]

The underlying idea is that perfectionism isn't just a personal habit or trait, but also a large-scale cultural phenomenon. At any given time, society's values shape the norms of all its institutions—families, schools, churches, and even political groups. Naturally, these institutions then affect individuals' values, beliefs, and personalities.

Thomas Curran and Andrew Hill, the authors of this meta-analysis, measured the generational change of specific types of perfectionism: self-oriented, socially prescribed, and other-oriented. Between 1989 and 2016, scores for all three types increased considerably.

- *Self-oriented perfectionism,* meaning an irrational drive for personal perfection, increased by 10%;

- *Socially prescribed perfectionism* increased by 32%, reflecting excessive expectations from others toward oneself;
- *Other-oriented perfectionism,* or a tendency to place unrealistic expectations on others, increased by 16%.

In other words, the rise of perfectionism is a three-fold problem. We expect too much from ourselves, we feel that society is increasingly demanding, and we place high expectations on others as well.

But why?

One possible explanation, proposed by Curran and Hill, is the influence of social media.

Platforms like Snapchat and Instagram allow users to publish and maintain a carefully curated public image of themselves. At the same time, constant exposure to the perfect self-representations of other people may intensify one's concerns about their body image, income, lifestyle, and professional success. In a virtual world where everyone tries to put up the best possible version of themselves, lacking in anything reinforces insecurities.

Another factor to consider is the meritocratic worldview that dominates modern culture.

Meritocracy (*merit,* from Latin *mereō,* and -*cracy,* from Ancient Greek κράτος [*kratos*] meaning *strength, power*) is the notion that anyone can achieve success, status, and the perfect lifestyle if they try hard enough.

While this sentiment may sound uplifting at first, it hides a downside as well. It implies that if you're not yet successful (wealthy, strong, or athletic), you're simply not trying hard enough. You lack true passion. Maybe you're not putting in enough effort. And you know what? You're also failing too often, too much. This dynamic increases performance pressure and fear of failure, leading to the perfect environment for overthinking.

When we still manage to push through and reach our goals despite the persistent thoughts, anxiety, analysis paralysis, and perfectionism, the results seem worth it. However, what's the real price that we pay?

The High Cost Of Being Perfect

Chasing excellence is often guided by the principle that *"the ends justify the means."* Let's take a moment to reflect on what we lose along the way and see if the price is truly worth it.

Self-critical perfectionism reduces motivation and leads to poor progress toward one's goals.[5] After all, falling short is part of the growth process. Harsh self-criticism in response to every mistake thwarts improvement and reinforces a fixed mindset with too much focus on achieving specific results rather than embracing a continuous journey of lifelong improvement.

Getting fixated on specific and unrealistic standards **may** *impair our ability to celebrate small wins and personal records.* Running your first mile without completely losing breath is a great achievement, but it fades in comparison to finishing a standard 26-mile marathon. Securing your first job in a new line of work deserves wholehearted respect, but this entry-level position may come with lower pay rates than the industry standard. Your perception of these achievements will depend on your focus.

Perfectionism and fear of failure also *reduce our ability to process and apply constructive criticism.* Someone with a growth mindset sees useful feedback as an opportunity for improvement. They don't perceive critique as a personal attack on their identity. For the overthinker and perfectionist, every piece of feedback is a sign of failure which they strive to avoid at any cost.

In its most extreme forms, perfectionism not only slows down progress and growth but also *delivers a heavy blow to mental health.* Studies have found an association between high perfectionism scores and the presence of self-harm or suicidal thoughts, especially those stemming from fear of humiliation.[6,7,8]

Perfectionism creates a hostile environment, almost unbearable at times. However, this doesn't mean that we should abandon all ambition and desire for success. The goal is to find a healthy middle ground between the extremes.

Find Your Goldilocks Zone

In the classic fairy tale *Goldilocks and the Three Bears*, a little girl finds her way into the house of an ursine family.

While the bears were away, Goldilocks tried the porridge from three bowls on the kitchen table. One was too hot, the second too cold, but the third one? It had just the right temperature, and Goldilocks ate it all. When she went upstairs to have a nap, she found out that Father Bear's bed was too rough, and Mama Bear's was the exact opposite—uncomfortably soft. Baby Bear's bed was perfect, and Goldilocks fell asleep in it.

Astronomers use the term *Goldilocks zone* or *circumstellar habitable zone* to describe the range of orbits around a star in which planets could have liquid water on their surface. Being closer to the star would evaporate the water. Being farther away would freeze it down. Both extremes are detrimental to life as we know it. The distance between the star and the planet has to be *just right*.[9]

You can use the Goldilocks zone concept as a mental model: Extremes are usually detrimental for all means and purposes. The most favorable results lie in the just right level of intensity.

From this perspective, dysfunctional perfectionism is just as detrimental as an extreme disregard for excellence. The former deprives us of effective learning, childlike curiosity, and the right to joyful experiments. At the same time, abandoning high standards, competitiveness, and ambition altogether can also be a recipe for stagnation and loss of opportunities.

Consistent productivity without sacrificing mental health

lies in the healthy middle ground between the extremes of perfectionism and apathy: in the Goldilocks zone.

Here are a few concepts that may help you find yours.

<u>Be Selective</u>

In <u>Chapter 5</u>, we explored the Pareto principle: 80% of outcomes come from just 20% of the causes. What are the vital few tasks that will bring you the bulk of the result?

By focusing your attention and energy on these endeavors, you'll be able to secure outstanding results without spending too much time overthinking. Contrary to that, losing yourself in a whirlpool of minor actions could devour your resources and still bring you just 20% of the desired outcome.

<u>Seek The Flow State</u>

In 1990, Hungarian-American psychologist Mihaly Csikszentmihalyi (pronounced *me-high chick-sent-me-high*) introduced the concept of flow. In psychology, this term refers to a highly focused state of mind that leads to exceedingly high productivity.[10]

Since the 1970s, athletes have had a different term for this: *being in the zone*. Arthur Ashe, one of the top tennis players at the time, explained it in the following words in a book based on his audio diaries:[11]

> *I thought I was playing unconscious, but Borg beat me 6-4, 7-6 tonight, and he is in what we call the*

zone. (That comes originally from Twilight Zone and translates, more or less, into Another World.) The kid has no concept of what he is doing out there—he is just swinging away and the balls are dropping in.

Being in the zone essentially means performing at the peak of your abilities, and focusing all your resources on a particular task. In this state, you lose a clear perception of the world beyond the activity at hand. Time ceases to exist. Emotions are dulled. Even the sense of self may be temporarily lost.

Distractions are wiped out, and the boost in productivity may be as high as 500%.[12]

Sounds almost magical. How do you even reach such a state?

At its core, it's all about finding the intersection between a high level of challenge and skill.

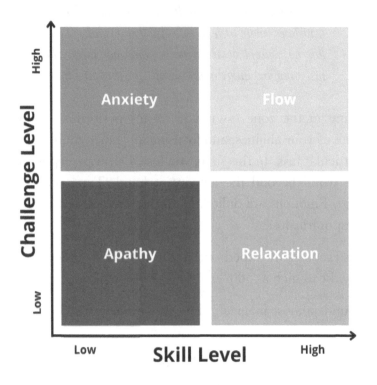

When you face an easy task with little to no related skills or background, *indifference and apathy* are the most likely outcomes. For example, imagine that you've never touched the violin in your life. One day, your friend hands you their instrument and asks you to play something. You could try for a while, but overall this experience wouldn't be stimulating or interesting for longer than a few minutes. At the same time, you probably wouldn't worry much about the situation, as it's not engaging.

When you take on a highly demanding task without the proper skill set to complete it, *anxiety* sets in. You expect troubles and failure ahead, as you know you're not prepared for a challenge of this magnitude. For example, let's say you're a beginner violinist who has to play in front of a full concert hall. The challenge is disproportionately significant compared to your current skill level. Worrying comes naturally in this situation.

Now, imagine that you're a professional violinist. You've been playing it since preschool, polishing your skills every day for several decades now. In this scenario, playing something as basic as the scales in a certain key no longer feels like practice. You're in full control. A low challenge level combined with significant skill and experience brings forth a sense of *relaxation*. Like a fish in water, you just enjoy the process and bask in a familiar environment.

To achieve the *flow* state, both the challenge and the skill level have to be substantially high, yet not overwhelming. For a professional violinist, this could be soloing Paganini's fiendishly difficult Caprice No.5 before hundreds of seasoned listeners. For a beginner who's just learning the ropes (or rather, strings), a similar experience could stem from playing in front of a small group of friends and family at a weekend gathering.

That's the intrinsic beauty of being in the zone: It grows with your experience and skills.

Perfectionism promises an idealized and largely unachievable result, with no regard for your current resources. The flow state is based on your resources and skills, putting them to work on a worthy challenge. It will be HARD, but also reachable if you mobilize all your efforts.

Practice Gratitude

"Here we go again, a gratitude journal? I've heard about it a hundred times!"

If that thought popped up in your mind, it's perfectly understandable.

Gratitude practices have become so mainstream in the self-improvement domain that many people don't take them seriously anymore. Clichés don't stick.

Here's the thing, though: Some techniques work precisely because they're basic. Think of them as foundational blocks for better thinking, just like proper hydration is essential for nutrition.

Deliberate gratitude shifts your focus from an unattained dream result to a small win on the path there. Instead of stressing out about not speaking fluent German yet, you celebrate your first two-minute conversation with the barista at a coffee shop in Berlin. It surely wasn't perfect, but it got the job done. It's a direct sign of your progress.

Besides fostering a mindset shift, practicing gratitude affects the brain's function directly. Whether it's in the form of thankful meditation or keeping a journal, studies reported tangible benefits from practicing gratitude.

- Gratitude meditation *improves self-motivation and helps you better process your emotions.* The effect is based on a regulation of the connectivity between the amygdala and the prefrontal cortex, parts of the brain that play a crucial role in decision-making, memory, and emotional response.[13]
- Gratitude as a personality trait has been *linked to better subjective sleep quality and duration.*[14]
- Writing down lists of recent events that you feel grateful for may *improve life satisfaction levels and reduce the intensity of perceived stress.*[15]

To get an idea of how gratitude could work, try going through the following one-minute exercise.

Start a 20-second timer and look around you for *GREEN* objects.

Plants, toys, office items, anything counts.

Check your desk, the windowsill, the walls, the clothes hanging on the chair. Notice those *GREEN* objects, even the tiniest ones.

Ready?

Are you sure?

100% confident?

Great!

Now, when the timer stops…

Without looking around again…

Name all the *RED* objects that you have nearby. Chances are, you'll have a hard time doing this. Your mind was focused on a different color.

A similar process happens with positive and negative events, failures and wins. When your mind is preoccupied with problems and fears, it misses out on the small achievements. Conversely, when you shift your focus to the joyful moments and small achievements even for a short while, you prime yourself to notice them more often around you.

So how do you practice gratitude and other techniques against perfectionism?

Action Steps

Start a gratitude journal. At the end of each day, set aside 5-15 minutes to make a short list of events, ideas, and interactions that you're grateful for. Give yourself a moment to relive them again in your mind. How do you feel about this day?

Enter the zone. The elusive flow state is notoriously hard to enter, but you can increase your chances of getting into it. Pick a task or activity that fits your skills and dial up the challenge until it feels barely reachable for your current level. Then, eliminate as many distractions as possible, get to work, and give it everything you've got. Make sure to pick a challenge that feels tough on a personal but not necessarily a global level. For example, if you usually do one-mile runs, try going for two miles, not straight to a marathon distance. If you usually write flash fiction under 1,000 words, put yourself to the test with a 1,500-word short story penned down in a single evening. The specifics of the challenge will vary wildly depending on your line of work and experience, but the general rule is to pick a goal that's barely out of reach and then focus all your resources on achieving it here and now. Will this guarantee you'll reach the zone? Not exactly. The flow isn't so much a destination, but rather a byproduct of your performance. Skillful work on a particularly tough task—that's the combination with the highest probability of leading you into the zone.

Adorn your scars with gold. Recall a recent mistake, failure, or unfortunate event. Consider it from different perspectives. Can you name a few reasons for appreciating it instead of feeling resentment, shame, or pain? Maybe it was a valuable, albeit unpleasant lesson. Or perhaps it opened the door to new possibilities and future growth. This is a delicate and potentially triggering topic, of course. Still, do your best to shift your perspective and find something worth appreciating in all chapters of your life story—even the painful ones.

Modern society relentlessly pursues ever-rising standards and increasingly unrealistic goals that spark overthinking and perfectionism. Pause for a while. Breathe in, breathe out. Look around.

Notice the shape of the clouds flying across the sky, thousands of miles above the ground. Are they perfect? No, not by any human standards. They're still glorious, within the framework of life itself.

What about a broken tea bowl? Some would say it's flawed and throw it away. Others will choose to give it a second life and find beauty in the way it was repaired—with love, attention, craftsmanship, and gold. The unique adventure of this tea bowl embodies the fleeting nature of all things. Imperfect, impermanent, incomplete. Wonderful, nonetheless.

Finding the balance between this wabi-sabi mindset and a desire for growth may be the ultimate solution to perfectionism.

And just like that, we reached the final stretch of our adventure through the realms of overthinking and productivity.

It's time for a quick wrap-up and a parting note.

Chapter Summary

- Overthinking is often based on an underlying fear of failure and its consequences, like harsh criticism. Perfectionism offers a misleading and unrealistic protection against failure.
- A healthier and more balanced approach lies in worldviews like the Japanese wabi-sabi, which

acknowledges the imperfection, incompleteness, and impermanence of all things.

- Studies reported that the global rates of perfectionism are on the rise. Factors contributing to this tendency include increased social media use and an increasingly competitive social environment.
- The cost of perfectionism is unaffordable. It includes impaired mental health, sub-optimal productivity, loss of motivation, and a decreased ability to celebrate small wins.
- Instead of chasing unachievable perfection, a more balanced approach could be based on specific productivity strategies like using the Pareto principle or trying to reach the flow state.
- Practice gratitude techniques to help your mind focus on the small wins and happy events that pave your progress.

AFTERWORD

No one is immune to overthinking, especially when it comes to productive work.

Of course, some people are more susceptible to it. You're probably one of them if you picked up this book. I am too.

While writing these chapters, I lost count of the instances when I slipped into overthinking, perfectionism, and all possible shades of anxiety.

"Are my words clear, useful, and well-chosen enough? Maybe I should trash everything, then start from the beginning? Do I have what it takes to be a writer?"

Luckily, this story has a bright side as well.

Can you guess what helped me break through the mental storm whenever I felt stuck?

The exact techniques that I shared with you. Not always on time. The result isn't even close to perfection. Still, we're here, steadily approaching the full stop of the final paragraph.

The fact that you're reading these words is a testament to the effectiveness of all the ideas that we explored together. They helped me tremendously—not only while writing this specific book, but also throughout hundreds of other projects. I hope you find these strategies useful too.

After all, the end goal of productivity is to bring value to other people and the world. When we allow overthinking, anxiety, analysis paralysis, and perfectionism to take over the mind, progress is impaired. Sometimes, it's abandoned altogether. We run as fast as possible and remain in the same place. We create no value, and we don't improve anyone's life.

Sure, the road to any meaningful result will be full of challenges.

Temporal traps lie ahead: portals to the past (rumination), fissures to the future (worrying). Weave your way through them. Bring your mind back to the present moment with techniques like attentional grounding and thought defusion.

Sometimes, you may struggle with an overabundance of choices that lead to analysis paralysis. Move on by following your core values. Remember that the cost of inaction may sometimes be higher than choosing anything, like a donkey dying from hunger between two piles of delicious hay.

Nurture a growth mindset that hungers for continuous improvement, not a specific result. Seek knowledge, not just passing a test. Strive for mastery, not just an incidental raise at work. As you keep growing, the small wins and marginal gains start to compound. A minuscule 1% improvement daily leads to massive results in the long run if you stay consistent.

And if you still find yourself under a vicious siege from persistent thoughts? Recall the white bear phenomenon: Trying to block out specific ideas from your mind leads to their paradoxical reinforcement. Instead, indulge them for a while or find a meaningful distraction. After some time, even the most relentless white bears go away.

Remember that your mind is like a thought toolbox. Fill it with actionable mental models, productivity boosters, and goal-setting strategies. Put them to use, track your progress, and stay patient. Like everything else in life, mastering these skills takes time and intention.

Do you feel overwhelmed and unable to keep up with the tidal way of incoming information? That's natural. Our brains are designed to get ideas, not store them! Build yourself an external brain system that perfectly fits the paradigm of the information age.

But most importantly, do your best to embrace imperfection and impermanence. Appreciate your life and work even (especially!) when they feel rough. After every fall, learn something new and move on. After every break, consider finding a way to mend the pieces instead of throwing everything out in resentment.

Even a shattered tea bowl can be turned into a work of art. Imperfect as everything else under the sun, but with a unique story to tell.

After you close this book, rest for a while. Don't jump right back into the fray.

When you eventually do, don't fear mistakes or focus too much on the outcome. Appreciate the process instead.

The only way to never fall is not to move at all, and I believe you have an exciting journey waiting for you.

What will your next step be?

OVER 10,000 PEOPLE HAVE ALREADY SUBSCRIBED. DID YOU TAKE YOUR CHANCE YET?

In general, around 50% of the people who start reading do not finish a book. You are the exception, and we are happy you took the time.

To honor this, we invite you to join our exclusive Thinknetic newsletter. You cannot find this subscription link anywhere else on the web but in our books!

Upon signing up, you'll receive two of our most popular bestselling books, highly acclaimed by readers like yourself. We sell copies of these books daily, but you will receive them as a gift. Additionally, you'll gain access to two transformative short sheets and enjoy complimentary access to all our upcoming e-books, completely free of charge!

This offer and our newsletter are free; you can unsubscribe anytime.

Here's everything you get:

✓ Critical Thinking In A Nutshell eBook **($9.99 Value)**
✓ The Intelligent Reader's Guide To Reading eBook **($9.99 Value)**
✓ Break Your Thinking Patterns Sheet **($4.99 Value)**
✓ Flex Your Wisdom Muscle Sheet **($4.99 Value)**
✓ All our upcoming eBooks **($199.80* Value)**

Total Value: $229.76

Go to thinknetic.net for the offer!

(Or simply scan the code with your camera)

SCAN ME

*If you download 20 of our books for free, this would equal a value of 199.80$

THE PEOPLE BEHIND THINKNETIC

Christoph Maurer, Founder and CEO

Christoph has always been a voracious reader with a writing talent. A bit less common, he has also been fascinated by business since he was a child. Consequently, after earning his degree in business management, he chose publishing as a full-time career. With his good friend of over 15 years, Michael, he founded Thinknetic. The company aims to build the most reader-centric original publishing house possible and become a household brand trusted by its dear readers. Practicing what he preaches, Christoph spends a considerable amount of time reading every day, deeply influenced by the examples set by Charlie Munger and Warren Buffet.

Michael Meisner, Founder and CEO

When Michael ventured into publishing books on Amazon, he discovered that his favorite topics—the intricacies of the human mind and behavior—were often tackled in a way that's too complex and unengaging. Thus, he dedicated himself to making his ideal a reality: books that effortlessly inform, entertain, and resonate with readers' everyday experiences, enabling them to enact enduring positive changes in their lives. Together with like-minded people, this ideal became his passion and profession. Michael is primarily in charge of steering the operational side of Thinknetic, as he continues to improve and extend the business.

Claire M. Umali, Publishing Manager

Collaborative work lies at the heart of crafting books, and keeping everyone on the same page is an essential task. Claire oversees all the stages of this collaboration, from researching to outlining and from writing to editing. In her free time, she writes online reviews and likes to bother her cats.

Farley Bermeo, Publishing Manager

Farley has a knack for storytelling and writing personal narratives, both mundane and the extraordinary. Combining his background in writing and experience in program management, he ensures that ideas are transformed into pages. He believes that a good story is better told with a steaming cup of coffee.

Ivan Kokhno, Writer

Ivan is an anesthesiologist turned writer and marketer. His main focus is crafting sales emails for health &

supplement brands, with content and book writing on the side as a personal passion. Ivan reads one book per week, sometimes out loud to his cat Ruby.

Andrew Speno, Content Editor

Andrew is a teacher, writer, and editor. He has published two historical nonfiction books for middle-grade readers, a biography of Eddie Rickenbacker and the story of the 1928 Bunion Derby ultra-marathon. He enjoys cooking, attending live theater, and playing the ancient game of go.

Sandra Agarrat, Language Editor

Sandra Wall Agarrat is an experienced freelance academic editor/proofreader, writer, and researcher. Sandra holds graduate degrees in Public Policy and International Relations. Her portfolio of projects includes books, dissertations, theses, scholarly articles, and grant proposals.

Ralph Escarda, Layout Designer

Ralph's love for books prevails in his artistic preoccupations. He is an avid reader of non-fictional books and an advocate of self-improvement through education. He dedicates his spare time to doing portraits and sports.

Alpia Villacorta, Layout Designer

Alpia makes sure that each book follows Thinknetic's formatting and design standards, helping it look outstanding, organized, and reader-friendly. She also helps curate suitable images for book covers. For Alpia, becoming an expert layout designer requires a lot of creativity and attention to detail. She believes that maintaining a positive and joyful attitude, along with reading self-help books, can aid in taking care of one's mental health.

Yusra Rafiq, Copywriter

Yusra Rafiq, a freelance content alchemist, crafts content across diverse niches. Her expertise, honed over three years, encompasses writing, SEO optimization, and a spectrum of digital content. Beyond work, Yusra finds joy in family, pets, and love for documentaries, true crime, and sci-fi.

Jemarie Gumban, Hiring Manager

Jemarie is in charge of thoroughly examining and evaluating the profiles and potential of the many aspiring writers and associates for Thinknetic. With an academic background in Applied Linguistics and a meaningful experience as an industrial worker, she approaches her work with a discerning eye and fresh outlook. Guided by her unique perspective, Jemarie derives fulfillment from turning a writer's desire to create motivational literature into tangible reality.

Evangeline Obiedo, Publishing Assistant

Evangeline diligently supports our books' journey, from the writing stage to connecting with our readers. Her commitment to detail permeates her work, encompassing tasks such as initiating profile evaluations and ensuring seamless delivery of our newsletters. Her love for learning extends into the real world—she loves traveling and experiencing new places and cultures.

REFERENCES

Introduction

1. Carroll, L., & Tenniel, J. (1999). *Through the looking-glass*. Dover Publications.

1. Your Brain Is A Time Machine

1. Mohd Azmi, N. A. S., Juliana, N., Azmani, S., Mohd Effendy, N., Abu, I. F., Mohd Fahmi Teng, N. I., & Das, S. (2021). Cortisol on circadian rhythm and its effect on cardiovascular system. *International Journal of Environmental Research and Public Health*, 18(2), 676. https://doi.org/10.3390/ijerph18020676
2. Scheer, F. A. J. L., Morris, C. J., & Shea, S. A. (2013). The internal circadian clock increases hunger and appetite in the evening independent of food intake and other behaviors. *Obesity*, 21(3), 421–423. https://doi.org/10.1002/oby.20351
3. Buonomano, D. (2017). *Your brain is a time machine: The neuroscience and physics of time*. W. W. Norton & Company.
4. World Health Organization. (2022). *ICD-11: International classification of diseases for mortality and morbidity statistics (eleventh revision)*. https://icd.who.int/browse/2024-01/mms/en
5. L'esprit de l'escalier. (2024, March 11). In *Wikipedia*. https://en.wikipedia.org/wiki/L%27esprit_de_l%27escalier
6. Smith, S. (2018, April 10). *5-4-3-2-1 coping technique for anxiety*. University of Rochester Medical Center. https://www.urmc.rochester.edu/behavioral-health-partners/bhp-blog/april-2018/5-4-3-2-1-coping-technique-for-anxiety.aspx
7. The Washington Center for Cognitive Therapy. (n.d.). *Cognitive defusion: An empirically supported strategy to change your relationship with problematic thoughts*. Retrieved April 2, 2024, from https://washingtoncenterforcognitivetherapy.com/cognitive-defusion/
8. Jyotirgamya. (n.d.). *Cognitive defusion techniques from ACT: How to distance yourself from unhelpful thoughts*. Retrieved April 2, 2024, from https://jyotirgamya.org/opinion/cognitive-defusion-technique-act/

2. Stuck In A Decision Deadlock?

1. Bogel, A. (2020). *Don't overthink it.* Baker Books.
2. Buridan's ass. (2023, September 7). In *Wikipedia.* https://en.wikipedia.org/wiki/Buridan%27s_ass
3. McAdam, Emma. (2023, February 22). *How to stop overthinking decisions.* Therapy in a Nutshell. https://therapyinanutshell.com/overthinking-decisions/
4. Schwartz, B. (2004). *The paradox of choice: Why more is less.* Ecco.

3. The 1% Advantage

1. Gilbert, E. (2016). *Big magic: Creative living beyond fear.* Riverhead Books.
2. Duhigg, C. (2017). *Smarter faster better: The transformative power of real productivity.* Random House Trade Paperbacks.
3. Dweck, C. S. (2007). *Mindset: The new psychology of success.* Ballantine Books.
4. Carol Dweck. (2016, January 13). What having a "growth mindset" actually means. *Harvard Business Review.* https://hbr.org/2016/01/what-having-a-growth-mindset-actually-means
5. Dweck, C. (2014, November). *The power of believing that you can improve* [Video]. TEDxNorrkoping. https://www.ted.com/talks/carol_dweck_the_power_of_believing_that_you_can_improve
6. Blackwell, L. S., Trzesniewski, K. H., & Dweck, C. S. (2007). Implicit theories of intelligence predict achievement across an adolescent transition: a longitudinal study and an intervention. *Child Development, 78*(1), 246–263. https://doi.org/10.1111/j.1467-8624.2007.00995.x
7. Nussbaum, A. D., & Dweck, C. S. (2008). Defensiveness versus remediation: self-theories and modes of self-esteem maintenance. *Personality & Social Psychology Bulletin, 34*(5), 599–612. https://doi.org/10.1177/0146167207312960
8. Mueller, C. M., & Dweck, C. S. (1998). Praise for intelligence can undermine children's motivation and performance. *Journal of Personality and Social Psychology, 75*(1), 33–52. https://psycnet.apa.org/record/1998-04530-003
9. Dweck, C. S. (2019). The choice to make a difference. *Perspectives on Psychological Science, 14*(1), 21–25. https://doi.org/10.1177/1745691618804180
10. National Cancer Institute. (n.d.). *Nerve tissue.* National Cancer

Institute SEER Training Modules. Retrieved April 2, 2024, from https://training.seer.cancer.gov/anatomy/nervous/tissue.html

11. Takagi, Y. (2016). History of neural stem cell research and its clinical application. *Neurologia Medico-Chirurgica*, *56*(3), 110–124. https://doi.org/10.2176/nmc.ra.2015-0340

12. Fares, J., Bou Diab, Z., Nabha, S., & Fares, Y. (2018). Neurogenesis in the adult hippocampus: History, regulation, and prospective roles. *International Journal of Neuroscience*, *129*(6), 598–611. https://doi.org/10.1080/00207454.2018.1545771

13. Sarrasin, J. B., Nenciovici, L., Foisy, L.-M. B., Allaire-Duquette, G., Riopel, M., & Masson, S. (2018). Effects of teaching the concept of neuroplasticity to induce a growth mindset on motivation, achievement, and brain activity: A meta-analysis. *Trends in Neuroscience and Education*, *12*, 22–31. https://doi.org/10.1016/j.tine.2018.07.003

14. Clear, J. (2018). *Atomic habits*. Avery.

15. Slater, M. (2012, August 8). Olympics cycling: Marginal gains underpin GB cycling dominance. *BBC Sport*. https://www.bbc.com/sport/olympics/19174302

4. The Wegner Experiment

1. Dostoevsky, F. (1997). *Winter notes on summer impressions*. Northwestern University Press

2. Wegner, D. M., Schneider, D. J., Carter, S. R., & White, T. L. (1987). Paradoxical effects of thought suppression. *Journal of Personality and Social Psychology*, *53*(1), 5–13. https://doi.org/10.1037//0022-3514.53.1.5

3. Wegner D. M. (1994). Ironic processes of mental control. *Psychological Review*, *101*(1), 34–52. https://doi.org/10.1037/0033-295x.101.1.34

4. Erskine, J. A. K., Georgiou, G. J., & Kvavilashvili, L. (2010). I suppress, therefore I smoke. *Psychological Science*, *21*(9), 1225–1230. https://doi.org/10.1177/0956797610378687

5. Hagerman, C. J., Stock, M. L., Beekman, J. B., Yeung, E. W., & Persky, S. (2021). The ironic effects of dietary restraint in situations that undermine self-regulation. *Eating Behaviors*, *43*, 101579. https://doi.org/10.1016/j.eatbeh.2021.101579

5. Choose Your Own Decision-Making Adventure

1. Pareto, V. (1896). *Cours d'économie politique professé à l'Université de Lausanne*. F. Rouge.

2. Juran. (2019, March 12). *Pareto principle (80/20 rule) & Pareto analysis guide*. https://www.juran.com/blog/a-guide-to-the-pareto-principle-80-20-rule-pareto-analysis/

3. Martins, A. L. A., Liska, G. R., Beijo, L. A., Menezes, F. S. de, & Cirillo, M. Â. (2020). Generalized Pareto distribution applied to the analysis of maximum rainfall events in Uruguaiana, RS, Brazil. *SN Applied Sciences*, *2*. https://doi.org/10.1007/s42452-020-03199-8

4. Rispoli, F. J., Zeng, S., Green, T., & Higbie, J. (2014). Even birds follow Pareto's 80-20 rule. *Significance*, *11*(1), 37–38. https://doi.org/10.1111/j.1740-9713.2014.00725.x

5. Clinical Excellence Commission. (n.d.). *Pareto charts & 80-20 rule*. NSW Government. Retrieved April 2, 2024, from https://www.cec.health.nsw.gov.au/CEC-Academy/quality-improvement-tools/pareto-charts

6. Rooney, P. (2002, October 3). Microsoft's CEO: 80-20 rule applies to bugs, not just features. *The Channel Company*. https://www.crn.com/news/security/18821726/microsofts-ceo-80-20-rule-applies-to-bugs-not-just-features

7. Bloch, A. (1980). *Murphy's law, book two: More reasons why things go wrong*. Price/Stern/Sloan Publishers.

8. Simon, H. A. (1956). Rational choice and the structure of the environment. *Psychological Review*, *63*(2), 129–138. https://uk.sagepub.com/sites/default/files/upm-binaries/25239_Chater~Vol_1~Ch_03.pdf

9. Simon, H. A. (1947). Administrative behavior: A study of decision-making processes in administrative organization (1st ed.). New York: Macmillan. OCLC 356505.

10. Eisenhower, D. (1954, August 19). *Address at the Second Assembly of the World Council of Churches, Evanston, Illinois*. https://web.archive.org/web/20150402111315/http://www.presidency.ucsb.edu/ws/?pid=9991

11. Mind Tools Content Team. (n.d.). *The Action Priority Matrix*. Retrieved April 2, 2024, from https://www.mindtools.com/agst6d0/the-action-priority-matrix

6. The 2-Minute Rule And Other Productivity Miracles

1. Nolen-Hoeksema, S., Wisco, B. E., & Lyubomirsky, S. (2008). Rethinking rumination. *Perspectives on Psychological Science*, *3*(5), 400–424. https://doi.org/10.1111/j.1745-6924.2008.00088.x
2. Cirillo, F. (2018). *The Pomodoro Technique: The acclaimed time management system that has transformed how we work.* Currency.
3. Leroy, S. (2009). Why is it so hard to do my work? The challenge of attention residue when switching between work tasks. *Organizational Behavior and Human Decision Processes*, *109*(2), 168–181. https://doi.org/10.1016/j.obhdp.2009.04.002
4. Tracy, B. (2017). *Eat that frog!: 21 great ways to stop procrastinating and get more done in less time.* Berrett-Koehler Publishers
5. Quoteresearch. (2013, April 3). *Eat a live frog every morning, and nothing worse will happen to you the rest of the day.* Quote Investigator. https://quoteinvestigator.com/2013/04/03/eat-frog/
6. Baumeister, R. F., Bratslavsky, E., Muraven, M., & Tice, D. M. (1998). Ego depletion: Is the active self a limited resource? *Journal of Personality and Social Psychology*, *74*(5), 1252–1265. https://doi.org/10.1037//0022-3514.74.5.1252

7. Is Your Brain At Full Capacity?

1. Miller, G. A. (1956). The magical number seven, plus or minus two: Some limits on our capacity for processing information. *Psychological Review*, *101*(2), 343–352. https://doi.org/10.1037/0033-295x.101.2.343
2. Allen, D. (2015). *Getting things done: The art of stress-free productivity.* Penguin Books.
3. Carroll, R. (n.d.). *Timeline.* Bullet Journal. Retrieved April 2, 2024, from https://bulletjournal.com/pages/about
4. Forte, T. (2023, November 23). *Building a second Brain: The definitive introductory guide.* Forte Labs. https://fortelabs.com/blog/basboverview/
5. Carroll, R. (2018). *The Bullet Journal method: Track the past, order the Present, design the future.* Portfolio.
6. Forte, T. (2022). *Building a second brain : A proven method to organize your digital life and unlock your creative potential.* Atria Books.

8. SMART Vs. PACT

1. Clear, J. (n.d.). *The goal is not the point.* James Clear. Retrieved April 2, 2024, from https://jamesclear.com/treasure-hunt
2. Duhigg, C. (2017). Smarter faster better: The transformative power of real productivity. Random House Trade Paperbacks.
3. Silvia, P. J., Jones, H. C., Kelly, C. S., & Zibaie, A. (2011). Trait self-focused attention, task difficulty, and effort-related cardiovascular reactivity. *International Journal of Psychophysiology, 79*(3), 335–340. https://doi.org/10.1016/j.ijpsycho.2010.11.009
4. Locke, E. A., & Latham, G. P. (1990). A theory of goal setting and task performance. *The Academy of Management Review, 16*(2), 480. http://dx.doi.org/10.2307/258875
5. Le Cunff, A. L. (n.d.) *SMART goals are not so smart: Make a PACT instead.* (2019). Ness Labs. Retrieved April 2, 2024, from https://nesslabs.com/smart-goals-pact

9. Ready To Transcend The Era Of Perfectionism?

1. Deng, C. (2024, March 30). *Kintsugi.* Brittanica. https://www.britannica.com/art/kintsugi-ceramics
2. Shannon number. (2024, January 23). In *Wikipedia.* https://en.wikipedia.org/wiki/Shannon_number
3. Powell, R. R. (2004). *Wabi sabi simple: Create beauty, value imperfection, live deeply.* Adams Media.
4. Curran, T., & Hill, A. P. (2019). Perfectionism is increasing over time: A meta-analysis of birth cohort differences from 1989 to 2016. *Psychological Bulletin, 145*(4), 410–429. https://doi.org/10.1037/bul0000138
5. Moore, E., Holding, A. C., Hope, N. H., Harvey, B., Powers, T. A., Zuroff, D., & Koestner, R. (2017). Perfectionism and the pursuit of personal goals: A self-determination theory analysis. *Motivation and Emotion, 42*, 37–49. https://doi.org/10.1007/s11031-017-9654-2
6. Gyori, D., & Balazs, J. (2021). Nonsuicidal self-injury and perfectionism: A systematic review. *Frontiers in Psychiatry, 12.* https://doi.org/10.3389/fpsyt.2021.691147
7. Hamilton, T. K., & Schweitzer, R. D. (2000). The cost of being perfect: Perfectionism and suicide ideation in university students. *Australian & New Zealand Journal of Psychiatry, 34*(5), 829–835. https://doi.org/10.1080/j.1440-1614.2000.00801.x

8. Pia, T., Galynker, I., Schuck, A., Sinclair, C., Ying, G., & Calati, R. (2020). Perfectionism and prospective near-term suicidal thoughts and behaviors: The mediation of fear of humiliation and suicide crisis syndrome. *International Journal of Environmental Research and Public Health, 17*(4), 1424. https://doi.org/10.3390/ijerph17041424

9. Alka, M. (n.d.). *Habitable zone.* Department of Mathematics & Astronomy, University Of Lucknow. Retrieved April 2, 2024, from https://www.lkouniv.ac.in/site/writereaddata/siteContent/202003291607135095alka_misra_Habitable_Zone.pdf

10. Csikszentmihalyi, M. (2008). *Flow: The psychology of optimal experience.* Harper Perennial Modern Classics.

11. Quoteresearch. (2016, September 16). *In the zone.* Quote Investigator. https://quoteinvestigator.com/2016/09/16/zone/

12. Gold, J., & Ciorciari, J. (2020). A review on the role of the neuroscience of flow states in the modern world. *Behavioral Sciences, 10*(9), 137. https://doi.org/10.3390/bs10090137

13. Kyeong, S., Kim, J., Kim, D. J., Kim, H. E., & Kim, J.-J. (2017). Effects of gratitude meditation on neural network functional connectivity and brain-heart coupling. *Scientific Reports, 7.* https://doi.org/10.1038/s41598-017-05520-9

14. Wood, A. M., Joseph, S., Lloyd, J., & Atkins, S. (2009). Gratitude influences sleep through the mechanism of pre-sleep cognitions. *Journal of Psychosomatic Research, 66*(1), 43–48. https://doi.org/10.1016/j.jpsychores.2008.09.002

15. Komase, Y., Watanabe, K., Hori, D., Nozawa, K., Hidaka, Y., Iida, M., Imamura, K., & Kawakami, N. (2021). Effects of gratitude intervention on mental health and well-being among workers: A systematic review. *Journal of Occupational Health, 63*(1). https://doi.org/10.1002/1348-9585.12290

DISCLAIMER

The information contained in this book and its components, is meant to serve as a comprehensive collection of strategies that the author of this book has done research about. Summaries, strategies, tips and tricks are only recommendations by the author, and reading this book will not guarantee that one's results will exactly mirror the author's results.

The author of this book has made all reasonable efforts to provide current and accurate information for the readers of this book. The author and their associates will not be held liable for any unintentional errors or omissions that may be found, and for damages arising from the use or misuse of the information presented in this book.

Readers should exercise their own judgment and discretion in interpreting and applying the information to their specific circumstances. This book is not intended to replace professional advice (especially medical advice, diagnosis, or treatment). Readers are encouraged to seek appropriate professional guidance for their individual needs.

The material in the book may include information by third parties. Third party materials comprise of opinions expressed by their owners. As such, the author of this book does not assume responsibility or liability for any third party material or opinions.

The publication of third party material does not constitute the author's guarantee of any information, products, services, or opinions contained within third party material. Use of third party material does not guarantee that your results will mirror our results. Publication of such third party material is simply a recommendation and expression of the author's own opinion of that material.

Whether because of the progression of the Internet, or the unforeseen changes in company policy and editorial submission guidelines, what is stated as fact at the time of this writing may become outdated or inapplicable later.

Thinknetic is committed to respecting copyright laws and intellectual property rights. We have taken reasonable measures to ensure that all quotes, diagrams, figures, images, tables, and other information used in this publication are either created by us, obtained with permission, or fall under fair use guidelines. However, if any copyright infringement has inadvertently occurred, please notify us promptly at wisdom-university@mail.net, providing sufficient details to identify the specific material in question. We will take immediate action to rectify the situation, which may include obtaining necessary permissions, making corrections, or removing the material in subsequent editions or reprints.

Made in United States
Troutdale, OR
07/30/2024